LONDON BOR

American
Basketry
and
Woodenware

# American Basketry and Woodenware

A COLLECTOR'S GUIDE

**William C. Ketchum, Jr.**

Macmillan Publishing Co., Inc.
New York

Collier Macmillan Publishers
London

To Aaron

**Library of Congress Cataloging in Publication Data**

Ketchum, William C., Jr. 1931-
    American basketry and woodenware.

    Bibliography: p. 215
    1. Basketwork—United States—Collectors and collecting. 2. Treenware—United States—Collectors and collecting. I. Title.
TS913.K47    746.4'1    73-6486
ISBN 0-02-562970-0

Copyright © 1974 by William C. Ketchum, Jr.

All rights reserved. No part of this book may be reproduced or transmitted in any form or by any means, electronic or mechanical, including photocopying, recording or any information storage and retrieval system, without permission in writing from the Publisher

Macmillan Publishing Co., Inc.
866 Third Avenue, New York, N.Y. 10022
Collier-Macmillan Canada Ltd.

First Printing 1974

Printed in the United States of America

# Contents

Preface   vii
Introduction   viii

## Basketry

Splint basketry   5
Splint household basketry   11
Farm and market baskets   21
Fisherman's basketry   31
Willow basketry   34
Straw basketry   41
Farm baskets   44
Miscellaneous basketry materials   46

## Woodenware

Wooden cooking ware   56
Baking utensils   77
Tableware   84
Washing and ironing utensils   95
Flax-spinning implements   105
Wool spinning and weaving   112

Sewing and embroidery treen 120
Decorated boxes 124
Utility boxes 132
Miscellaneous household treen 137
Water-drawing and storage vessels 150
Butter-making implements 155
Cheese manufacture 164
Apple preparation 170
Maple sugar equipment 175
Wooden farm implements 179

Appendix 193
Bibliography 215
Index 221

# Preface

A word about the scope of this book. When one speaks of American woodenware or basketry, it should be with the idea in mind that two distinct areas are involved: Indian-made ware and the ware produced by white settlers from the seventeenth century on. While certain forms are common to both groups, the variety and range of types is far greater among the settlers.

Several texts have dealt with Indian baskets and hand-formed wooden utensils, but less has been done in the colonial field, particularly in regard to basketwares. Accordingly, it is the purpose of this volume to discuss the numerous treen and basket forms developed and used by various groups of emigrants throughout the United States. Like any other general work, it cannot cover every device or every artisan. It must be viewed as a starting point from which serious students may begin to examine the primitive heritage of their own areas.

In this, as in prior work, I have been most ably assisted by the research staffs of the New York Historical Society and the New York Public Library to whom I, once again, extend my sincere thanks.

Most of the photographs for this work were taken by J.J. Smith of the Graduate Program, New York State Historical Society, Cooperstown. Mr. Smith's unfailing courtesy and cooperation have, in a very large part, made this project feasible. I wish, also, to express my appreciation to Todd Weinstein and Robert Day, who did the remainder of the illustrations, as well as to the various historians and librarians throughout the country who supplied information on the topics covered.

# Introduction

The anonymous nature of American basketry and woodenware belies its importance, both to those who once used it and to modern students of our country's past social customs. For decades collectors have gathered and studied the creations of ancient silversmiths, potters, and glassblowers. This work has been greatly facilitated by the fact that many such artisans marked at least a portion of their ware with a name or location relating to its manufacture. The basketmaker and the cooper seldom felt constrained to identify their products, making it most difficult to develop a coherent picture of these crafts.

Yet, there can be no doubt that, at least prior to 1800, far more utensils were produced in these media than in pottery, glass, or metal. The new land abounded in forests; any man with an axe and a knife could rough out enough tools and receptacles to supply his family. If finer or more complex pieces were desired, the local cooper or carpenter could supply them. It is hardly surprising, then, to learn that nearly every object produced in another medium was also attempted in wood or basketry materials. Glass goblets, china teacups, brass candlesticks—all these were duplicated in treen. Steel fish traps and ironstone bread trays had their woven splint counterparts. Our modern washing machines, meat grinders, and water coolers were all first manufactured from wood. In many cases, the medium proved unsuitable and was soon abandoned. However, such things as bowls and boxes are still made from the same substance employed by early workers.

Unfortunately, however, anything made in such abundance and so inexpensively tends to be held in low esteem. With the passage of time many handcrafted items in treen or basketry ceased to be of use or value to their owners. Chargers, porringers, noggins, dolly pins, and bee skeps, along with countless other items, became obsolete. Without a function and lacking the intrinsic value of silver or porcelain, they were assigned to the woodbin or left to rot in an attic or barn. Other fragile utensils, particularly basketware, were soon destroyed in the course of normal use. As a result, many early objects in these materials are gone, with nothing but obscure references in ancient books to indicate the nature or intended use of the tool.

However, it is possible to learn at least something of these articles and the people who made them. Local histories often contain notes, particularly during the great biographical period of 1860–1890, about community industries and prominent craftsmen. A precious few baskets and wooden utensils bear the carved, stamped, or stenciled name of a manufacturer. In some cases a reliable family history may accompany an artifact. These references may be traced and, possibly, a man and his work may be brought to light. Once certain pieces have been identified as the work of a given cooper or basket weaver, others bearing similar characteristics—an unusual finial or a particular finish—may be attributed to him. The work is tedious and often leads only to a dead end, but it is a most important part of our country's social history that is being examined. It is precisely this desire for knowledge that sets the true antiquarian apart from the mere accumulator.

# Basketry

At Bridgewater, in the far northeastern corner of Maine, a small shingle house stands beside busy U.S. Route 1. It is the home of John Newell, basketmaker. His wares, primarily ash splint baskets of various shapes and sizes, hang in rows about the building, and throughout the summer, tourists stop to talk and to buy.

To many, no doubt, he and his trade are curiosities, quaint anachronisms in a busy industrial society. Yet, within this century, many others followed the craft, not only in Maine, but throughout the United States. The first settlers brought with them baskets and basket-making skills utilized for centuries on the Continent. The Indians, whose lands the settlers took, were also basketmakers, employing a wide variety of techniques and materials.

In the decades following first colonization, white and Indian manufacturing techniques changed as each group adopted designs employed by the other. Consequently, with the exception of certain Indian styles, such as those of the Southwest, which have survived basically intact, the term *Indian Basket* is a misnomer. Economic conditions and, perhaps, a natural inclination explain the fact that most of our present-day traditional basketmakers are Indians (large numbers of baskets are still manufactured on reservations), but the containers the Indians create are, for the large part, indistinguishable from those produced by whites.

Present-day interest in early basketry is not unique. As early as the 1890s, at a time when traditional basketmaking was fading before the onslaught of mass-produced containers, a craft revival led to basket classes, basket schools, and "how to" books, all directed primarily at the middle-class hobbyist. Much of the ware produced at that time is now considered antique and collectible.

In fact, the term *antique* must be applied with some flexibility in this area. Due to their fragile nature, few pre-nineteenth-century baskets exist, and most date within the last hundred years. Moreover, since traditional forms changed slowly, and since these containers are seldom marked or dated, it is difficult to assign a specific period to most.

There are, however, certain general guides to age. Accessory materials, bindings, and fittings changed over the years. The earliest baskets were, where necessary, held together with natural substances: bark, thin strips of wood, or even animal sinew. Nails employed were handwrought or of the square-headed "cut" variety. By mid-nineteenth century, thread, string, or imported organic material such as raffia was being used for binding. The introduction of wire nails, metal bail handles, and tin bracing indicated further concessions to modern methods.

Basketmaking materials also underwent modification. Early splint or willow was hand-cut, thick, rough, and irregular. The widespread use of veneer cutting machinery led, by 1900, to thinner, uniform elements.

Handles were, at first, carved by hand. These, and other solid components of the baskets tended to be irregular and to show the tool marks left by the people who carefully whittled them out. Later lifts were pressed or die cut and were monotonously similar.

While differences in the craftsman's skills created exceptions (there have always been good and bad basketmakers), there was a general decline in style and construction in the late nineteenth and early twentieth centuries. The individual worker, pressed by factory competition, tried to adopt his enemy's methods and, of course, failed. Lacking the ability to produce cheaply and in volume, he turned to novelty items—souvenir baskets and the like—which are today his main output.

# Splint basketry

The majority of American baskets, antique and contemporary, are made of splint—thin, flexible strips of wood, generally from oak, ash, hickory, or poplar trees. The first settlers found Indian basketmakers working in this medium—one with which they were also familiar.

Preparation of basket splint involved several time consuming steps. A young tree, with a minimum of knots, was felled in winter when the sap was not flowing, sectioned, then stored under water. When well soaked, each piece was stripped of bark and branch and, then while still water softened, hammered throughout its length with wooden clubs or mallets. This process caused the wood to separate along the annular growth rings. The semicircular portions of trunk were then split into "rivings," strips approximately two by three inches and some three feet long. This splitting was accomplished by use of a riving chisel or froe, an iron knife blade with triangular edge and handle set in at a right angle, which was hammered into the end of each block with a wooden mallet or froe club. The rivings thus produced were further subdivided into "splints" about one-half inch thick either by pounding or by shaving with a draw knife, a narrow double-handled blade.

These splints, also known as splits, were the raw material from which many an early basket was woven. Soaked in water to promote flexibility, they were formed into a wide variety of shapes. The basic technique employed was plaiting. Two sets of elements (the weft and the warp) were passed alternately over and under one another to create an interlocking surface. This plaiting was of two sorts—crosshatching and hexagon weaving.

A typical crosshatch-weave splint basket is shown in figure 1.

*Figure 1.*

The technique is not difficult. The weaver starts with four pieces of splint laid crosswise and adds more until a suitable bottom size is obtained. Then he turns up the ends of the splits and weaves in horizontal strips known as "fills." When the vessel is tall enough, the split ends above the top edge are trimmed to a point and turned down under a lower ring of fills. The top edge of the basket is itself formed of one or two hand-carved hoops, usually of hickory or ash. These are bound to the highest fill with thinner strips of "finish split." Handles in the shape of a horseshoe with tapered ends are set into the upper edge of the basket. They have a notch across the throat that locks into the top hoop. Smaller editions of these fixed handles were also used as anchors for free-swinging bail handles. Several variations may be seen among the baskets illustrated.

The crosshatch basket has advantages—its simplicity and its speed of construction. Consequently, it is the more commonly found. It also has two substantial disadvantages. The right-angle joinings slip readily, making for a weak and fragile container. Also, it requires a maximum amount of raw material.

These problems are resolved through use of the hexagon weave. Here the starting point is two splits laid crosswise in the

Splint basketry 7

form of an X. Into the upper and lower crotches thus formed, two more strands are laid, creating other crotches that are similarly filled until a bottom of satisfactory size is created. The splits are then turned up and the sides woven in the same manner. The top edge is finished in much the same way as was the crosshatch basket. As may be seen from figure 2, the result is a loosely interlaced framework with six-sided openings. The splits, being locked at all angles, do not slip. Understandably, this form was used either for vessels in which relatively large objects were carried or for those, such as clam baskets, where it was important to have ample drainage. Basketry in the hexagon pattern is relatively rare today.

Both design types were made either freehand or on basket molds. In the former case, the craftsman marked out a pattern in chalk on the shop floor. In the latter he might have used a variety of molds, some round, some square or oblong. While many of these were carved from solid wood (with applied carrying sticks they looked like giant tops), others were put together with staves like a barrel so that they would weigh less.

*Figure 2.*

Whether or not he used molds, the basketmaker generally worked at a stool (fig. 3) or table upon which the basket was placed so it could be turned during construction. This stool and a sharp knife were the major tools employed.

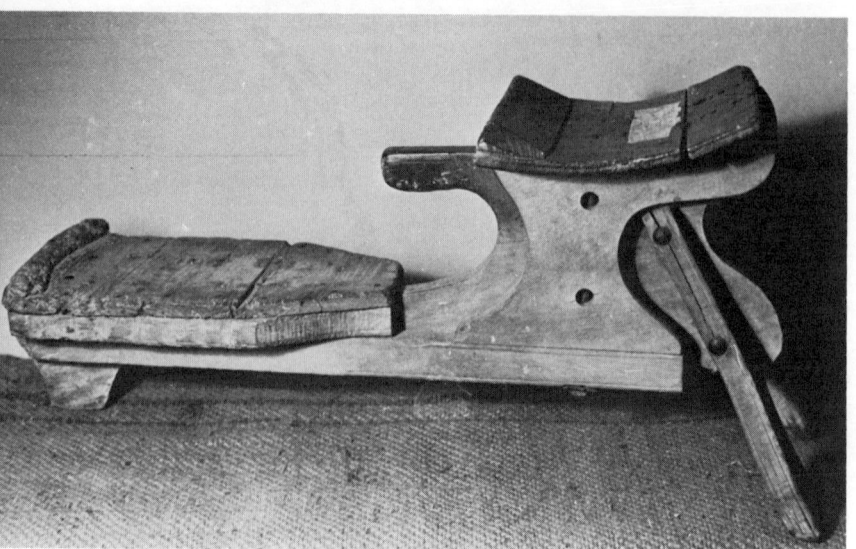

*Figure 3.*

Splint containers are more often than not found undecorated. Occasionally the natural brown or tan wood surface may be painted entirely blue, red, or yellow. Also, both Indian and white craftsmen used small stamps made from wood, cork, or corncob to enliven the surface with a pattern of circles, stars, squares, or leaves. These designs are seldom in more than two colors and appear most commonly on crosshatch basketry (see fig. 4). Later commercial baskets were also decorated by use of prestained fills, which could be woven in to provide a band or more of color. Examples of this technique appear in figures 5 and 6.

FIGURE 4 *Splint utility baskets with polychrome decoration.*

*Figure 5.*

FIGURE 6 *Splint utility baskets.*

Much of the charm associated with early basketry relates to individuality. No two baskets are ever quite alike even where made by the same person. It is this uniqueness that sets the hand-formed container apart from its mass-produced descendants. When David Cook of New Haven, Connecticut, patented the first basket-making machine, he sounded the death knoll for this diversity. The introduction of steam chambers to soften splint, veneer cutters to shape it, and stapling machines to bind it led to a uniform and uniformly dull product.

The factory basket is characterized by very wide and thin splint, wire bail handles, and pinnings of wire nail or staple. Some of the pre-1900 examples adhere to archaic forms and may be of interest to the collector despite the lack of individual touch. Since, in the interest of advertising, many of these containers were stamped with the manufacturer's name and/or address, they also have a specific historic reference generally lacking in the earlier work. They are serviceable and durable. Their failure is on another level and, as such, is a reflection of the general monotony inherent in mass-produced objects.

# Splint household basketry

Even today baskets play a role in the household, primarily in the form of receptacles for clothing and wastepaper. A hundred years ago a much wider variety of woven splint objects was used in the home. Cooking, cleaning, and cloth manufacturing all required specific forms. Many of these are now lost, but a few recognizable pieces have come down to us.

## Clothes hampers and baskets

Traditionally, families, particularly those in rural areas, held washday once a month. This led to substantial interim accumulations of soiled clothing, which were stored in a variety of clothes hampers. These containers ranged in height from two feet to over three feet and were square or rectangular. Such hampers were woven in the crosshatch pattern, generally with a matching cover (see fig. 5). Splint clothes hampers are uncommon, the preferred material being willow.

Clothes baskets, in which the wet wash was placed, were much more common. The one shown in figure 1 is of crosshatch woven ash splint and is four feet long by three feet wide. The lifts at each end clearly indicate that it was to be carried by two people. The basket lacks any structural reinforcement other than the top hoop and could never have been used for farm produce or other rough jobs.

A "Cloathes Baskett" of unknown form appears in a 1750 estate inventory, and the basketmaker Joseph Codding of Danielson, Connecticut, was selling them for fifty cents each in 1868.

## Bedbaskets and cradles

Though now uncommon, splint infant beds and cradles were no doubt once quite plentiful. Reference to a "Child bed Basket" appears in the inventory of the Reverend Ebenezer Thayer, who died at Roxbury, Massachusetts, in 1732, and the light weight and portability of such a crib must have appealed strongly to the crowded colonial family. The cover of the example illustrated (fig. 7) is of two parts: the foot, which is permanently attached, extending to the infant's shoulders, and a removable top. Since the loose splint weave allows for ample circulation of air, this portion of the cover could be placed over the child's face during the cold New England winters.

A few ovoid receptacles designated cradle baskets have also come to light. One of these, in the collection of Carl Hopf, is some forty inches long by twenty-six inches wide and is loosely crosshatch woven in a form not unlike a half watermelon. It is from Ohio.

*Figure 7.*

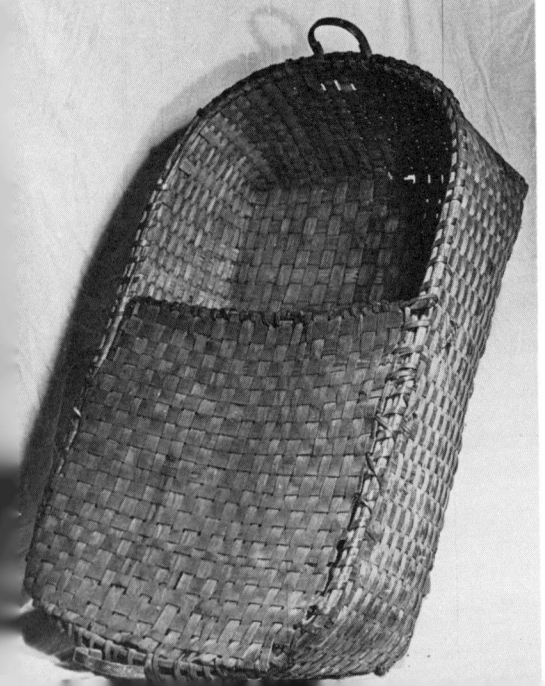

## Featherbed basket

Another bedroom accessory was the featherbed basket pictured in Gould's *Early American Wooden Ware*. During the warm months when there was no need for the bulky featherbeds and comforters, they were stored in a squat, circular container with a close-fitting top. This apple-shaped piece of closely cross-woven splint was three feet in diameter and three and a half feet high. The uncommon form may be recognized by the bowl-shaped cover that extends down over nearly half of the basket's surface.

## Chip and wood baskets

In the earliest days and for many years thereafter, wood was the major fuel used throughout the United States. Logs were cut into sizes suitable for stove or fireplace and placed nearby, often in a sturdy wood basket. Strongly woven with thicker than average splits and sturdy hickory handles, these containers were frequently three feet high and better than two feet wide. They are still made and used in certain areas of New England.

A related item was the open-faced chip basket, intended to carry and store wood fragments picked up around the chopping block and used to start fires. Shaker craftsmen made this form with leather linings, and it is still sufficiently common to appear in modern living rooms as a magazine holder or, worse, as a log carrier. In the latter capacity its unreinforced body and delicate handle soon break down.

## Charcoal sieves and baskets

Another common colonial fuel was charcoal used for summer cooking as well as in the numerous distilleries. Charcoal makers sifted their produce to remove foreign bodies and also to grade it by size. Consequently, sieves with various-sized splint mesh bottoms may be found. Generally, they are about two feet square with low, tightly woven sides and loose crosswoven bottoms. Some are reinforced across the base with wooden strips.

Both charcoal and coal were transported and stored in large circular baskets with metal band reinforcements. These often have inset handles or finger holds made by terminating the weave in two locations just below the top hoop. Charcoal baskets were similar to field or produce baskets and, unless telltale dust or fragments remain, may be confused with their more numerous cousins.

## Wastepaper baskets

A much later innovation is the wastepaper basket. It was many years before the colonists had paper that might be considered waste, and the form is of Victorian origin persisting to the present time. Arthur Corliss of South Tamworth, New Hampshire, was making wastepaper baskets by hand as late as the 1930s, cutting down his own ash trees and putting the pieces together without use of nails. His vase-shaped basket tapered down from top to bottom and was less than two feet tall.

## Flax, wool, and loom baskets

The preparation of material from flax or wool was a constant occupation of the rural housewife, and splint receptacles played their part. Cleaned flax fibers were stored in a flax basket prior to being hatcheled (this process is described in the section on woodenware). This basket was approximately a foot high and six inches square, and had a loosely wrapped splint loop handle (see fig. 8). A more popular version of this receptacle was made in willowware.

The stout-footed basket shown in figure 9 is of a type long known as wool baskets. From contemporary accounts they

FIGURE 8 Left to right, *splint egg basket, splint field basket, splint school or utility basket.*

have been associated with the process of cleansing wool prior to spinning. Some sources suggest that they were used as vessels into which raw wool was placed while being rinsed. The ash feet also raise the possibility that wool was dried in these baskets, as they would enable air to circulate freely around the material.

*Figure 9.*

## Basketry

The weaver also used a splint container, the loom basket. A late version with wide splints cut on a veneer machine is seen in figure 10. The high-stepped back is a trademark of this form. Some examples have as many as seven steps; and, generally, the more steps, the older the basket. Loom baskets were hung on a loom corner post and served as a receptacle for the thread bobbins used in weaving.

FIGURE 10   Left, *factory-made covered market basket;* right, *splint loom basket.*

### Mending baskets

Mending, sewing, or knitting baskets as they were variously termed, were a commonplace item in nineteenth-century homes and many are still in use. Most common is the decorated willow with double-lift top. However, a circular or oblong splint mending basket with hickory handle and top is also known. The example shown (fig. 8) has lost its cover but otherwise illustrates the type.

## Fruit-drying trays and baskets

Dried fruit, primarily apples (though pears were also preserved in this fashion), was a staple of the farm diet for many years. After being cored and sliced, the apples were laid out in a basket or tray to dry, preferably in the sun but often beside the fireplace or in a warm attic.

A wide variety of such trays are known. The two illustrated in figures 11 and 12 are of the shallow nonhandled form. In construction they are similar, in size very different. One is

*Figure 11.*

*Figure 12.*

four feet long, the other just over a foot. Both are lightly made of unreinforced, loosely cross-woven ash splint and probably were movable only when empty. The sides are very low, only an inch high in the smaller example, twice that in the other. Addition of a low handle would convert these trays to baskets but would in no way alter their use. Handled baskets of this form are less often found, probably because the lift interfered with storage and served no useful purpose.

Least common of all fruit dryers is the cobweb rack. This is circular in form and turns on a wooden center post. It is made of hickory strips extending out from the central rod about which long slivers of splint have been woven over and under, giving the appearance of a round cobweb. This rack was hung from the ceiling near a fireplace where, under influence of the rising heat, it slowly revolved, ensuring all fruit an equal drying time. Although an example was illustrated in Gould's *Early American Wooden Ware*, I have never seen another and the form must be considered extremely rare.

### Food storage hampers

Dried fruit, grain, and similar substances were often stored in food hampers or "mitchin boxes," which were square or circular, slightly shouldered, splint receptacles with tight-fitting cov-

FIGURE 13  *Decorated splint food-storage hamper.*

ers. The one pictured in figure 13 is late nineteenth century, made with wide veneer splint some of which has been stained to provide contrasting light and dark vertical banding. Such hampers often had a capacity of ten to fifteen bushels.

**Vinegar funnel**

Another uncommon object in splint is the funnel. Woven solidly in crosshatch technique, this cone-shaped utensil was used both in the kitchen and in vinegar and cider preparation. Gould illustrates one eighteen inches long, tapering down from a thirteen-inch mouth. Being both extremely fragile and unsuitable for the purpose, splint funnels were quickly replaced with tin or wood whenever the latter became available.

**Utility baskets**

Shown in figure 4 are representatives of the large group known as utility baskets. The term is generally applied to the sturdy square-bottomed example illustrated in figure 14, but many other types, with or without handles, deep and shallow, exist. They must have served a wide variety of purposes about the house: storage containers, table baskets for fresh fruit, scrap baskets, and the like. Unfortunately, in most cases the specific

FIGURE 14   *Splint clothes hamper.*

purpose, if any, is now lost. A number of basket manufactories including the Hibband Basket Co., of South Butler, New York, and Walter Moses and Co., of San Francisco, produced utility baskets.

# Farm and market baskets

Work in the fields and about the barns required a great many basket forms. The gathering of produce alone brought into play an array of these. Processing and preserving food involved other basketry.

### Sower's baskets

A small splint basket with broad bottom and mouth just wide enough to admit a man's hand was used by farmers when sowing seeds. A stout splint or leather loop attached to the rim of the vessel was secured to the worker's belt, enabling him to use both hands.

### Winnowing fan and sieve

Following harvest, it was necessary to separate the grain from the chaff. From the earliest days a splint winnowing fan or "wheat riddle" was used for this purpose. The fan was generally in the shape of a large ellipse as long as a man's reach and had two handle grips, which gave it somewhat the appearance of a giant scoop. A less familiar type was the winnowing basket, which differed in being a true ovoid rather than having the flattened front characteristic of the fan. Both forms were used in the same manner. Cut grain was first beaten with a flail (see Woodenware section) to dislodge the kernels from the heads. Then the mixture was placed in the fan and tossed into the air in a windy place. The wind action separated the lighter chaff from the grain.

Few extant fans are of great age. The hard treatment they received guaranteed an early demise. Yet, there can be no

FIGURE 15 Left, *grain winnowing sieve;* right, *small cider cheese press.*

doubt that the form is ancient. One was among the possessions of Captain Hopestill Foster, of Suffolk County, Massachusetts, inventoried in 1676.

After fanning, grain was sifted in a winnowing sieve similar to that shown in figure 15. This article is characteristically of circular oaken frame (for durability) with ash splint bottom. A few rectangular or square examples are also known.

## Field baskets

Splint produce baskets, known as *Schiene Korbe* among the Pennsylvania Dutch, were made in many varieties to transport or store vegetables. These containers ranged in size from one-half peck to two bushels. Two in the half-bushel size were listed in the estate of John Buttolph of Wethersfield, Connecticut, in 1692, while a half-peck example was inventoried at the death of Stephen Brewer of Roxbury, Massachusetts, in 1770.

## Farm and market baskets 23

The earliest version was oblong with inset handles and of thick cross-woven splint. By mid-nineteenth century circular baskets had become popular. These had a handle across the middle in the smaller sizes (up to one-half bushel) and a lifting handle, either inset or free standing, at each side in the larger versions (fig. 16).

The round baskets were made uniformly enough to allow for "nesting," and various sizes might be stacked conveniently, one inside the other. They were also often reinforced for heavy loads by wood or metal strapwork across the bottom.

*Figure 16.*

To meet the needs of an agricultural economy, millions were produced. In the late nineteenth century the Selleck basket works at Pound Ridge, New York, was selling field baskets at the following prices: peck size, $1.50 per dozen; half bushel, $2.16 per dozen; bushel, $3.00 per dozen. Prices in other areas of the country were comparable.

Today's factory-made bushel basket, wire-handled and of wide-cut splint, is the descendant of these early field or produce baskets.

## Fruit baskets

Closely allied in function to the produce container was the fruit or berry basket. The earliest of these were something less than a quart in capacity, narrow and deep with loop handles for attaching to the picker's belt. This was no doubt the form of the "three fruit basket" listed in Ebenezer Pierpoint's estate, assessed at Roxbury, Massachusetts, in 1768.

This form was replaced in the nineteenth century by a circular splint container with two loop handles. It looked much like a miniature bushel basket. In 1864 the Beecher Basket Company of Westville, Connecticut, patented a machine veneer version of this called the "Star" fruit basket. The Star came in half pint, pint, and quart sizes.

In the 1870s the round container was superseded by the "Delaware," another mass-produced basket but of square shape (see fig. 17). The pine-bottomed, basswood-sided Delaware was the forerunner of contemporary berry baskets. A collapsible version was developed by Charles Converse of Dubuque, Iowa, in 1864.

So that the bottom berries would not be crushed, these receptacles were seldom made in larger than two-quart size, and most are a quart or less in capacity. The earliest patent baskets are of interest to collectors, particularly where stamped with the manufacturer's mark.

*Figure 17.*

## Cheese baskets

Cheese or curd baskets used in the manufacture of cheese (see Woodenware section) are another interesting rural form. A typical example is shown in figure 2. A similar object is listed among the possessions of Thomas Dudley, who died in Roxbury, Massachusetts, in 1769. Cheese baskets were made of hickory or ash splint with straight or tapered sides and normally in a hexagonal weave, though cross-woven examples are known. Some were as large as two feet in diameter. Joseph Codding was producing cheese baskets in the 1870s, and the Shakers sold them for $1 each in 1833. The introduction of commercial cheese factories made this object obsolete.

## Egg baskets

Most farmers kept chickens, so an egg basket was indispensable in gathering and transporting the eggs. The basket shown in figure 18 is of cross-woven splint with a "kick-up" base to reduce pressure on the lower layers. It holds about two dozen eggs. This receptacle was also commonly made in hexagonal weave. Both styles had fixed or swinging center bail handles.

In the South, the Kentucky egg basket has been made for generations. Woven of split oak, it has a flat surface intended to rest against the side of a horse or a mule and is otherwise ovoid, sloping in toward the top. At one time these baskets were made to such exact specifications that they accommodated exactly one or two dozen eggs. The black basketmaker Levi Eye of Pendleton County, West Virginia, specialized in these. He is said to have made over 7,000 baskets in various forms.

*Figure 18.*

Farm and market baskets 27

## Ox muzzles and feed bags

There was even limited use of basketry in animal husbandry. Basketlike ox muzzles of ash splint were used to prevent the animals from eating grain while working the fields.

Less common are urn-shaped feed bags of tight cross-woven splint with hickory hoops bound into their foot-wide mouths. These fragile containers received hard usage, and only a few have survived to the present time.

## Goose baskets

Shown in figure 19 is a tall ovoid receptacle of a class known as goose baskets from their traditional association with goose plucking.

Down and feathers from domestic and wild geese were used to make pillows and feather beds. The birds were plucked

FIGURE 19 Left, *splint goose basket;* right, *splint sower's basket.*

## Basketry

two or three times a year, and the basket was placed over their heads to prevent the angry creatures from nipping their tormentors. The usual association of a matching lid raises the possibility that the down might also have been stored in the baskets.

## Pigeon baskets

Another exploited bird was the pigeon, both the domestic variety and the now extinct passenger pigeon. Until prevented from doing so by law, sportsmen held periodic shoots at which pigeons were set loose to serve as flying targets.

The birds were carried to shoots in woven splint baskets, two types of which are known. The first is a rectangular box with a bail handle and a trap door at each end large enough to permit entry of a hand and exit of a pigeon. A second type was circular with a single top opening. Both are shown in figure 20. The latter is a New Jersey form of particularly fine design. The unusual container seen in figure 21 may also have been used to transport pigeons or other domestic fowl, though its function is uncertain.

FIGURE 20 *Splint pigeon-carrying baskets.*

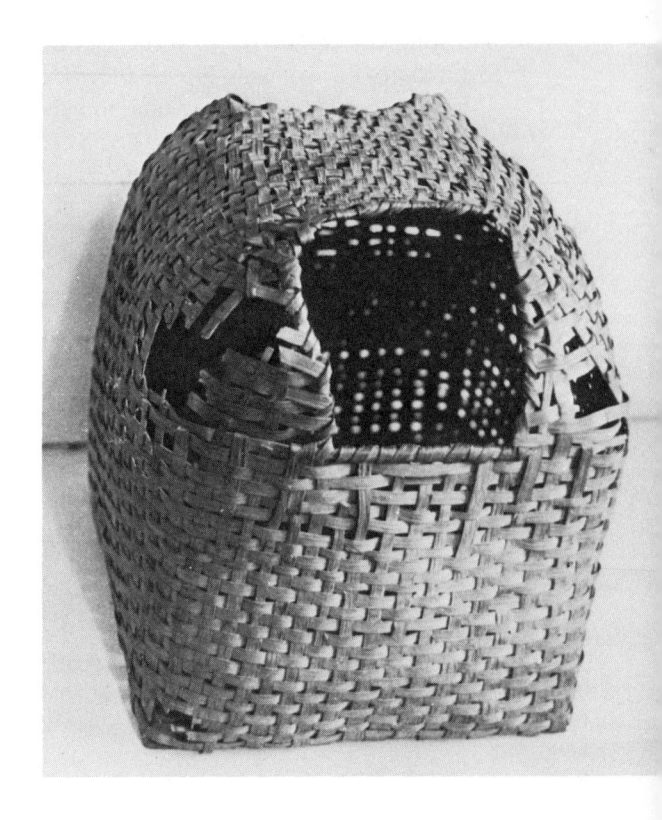

*Figure 21.*

## Market baskets

Various types were encompassed under the term *market basket*, including the classic oblong open basket with center lift, most commonly seen beneath the arm of Little Red Riding Hood. A covered version was advertised in the L. H. Mace and Co. of New York, New York, catalog of 1883. It was offered in four sizes from $3.00 to $5.50 per dozen.

An ovoid variation, the melon-shaped basket, was made by Corliss, and in the Southern highlands this was modified by indenting the center rib to form a two-lobe basket that fitted firmly across a woman's hip as she rode horseback to market.

In 1903, Jennie Hill, writing for the *Southern Workman*, noted that: "no better farm baskets were ever made than these same melon shaped mountain baskets, balancing as they do on the hip or across the neck of a horse in front of the rider. It is the boast of some of the most skilful old basket makers that their baskets will hold water, and it is an actual fact that they are sometimes so closely woven that meal can be carried in them."

Both Silas Nicholson of Oldrag, Virginia, and Bird Owsley of Vest, Kentucky, were still producing "hip" baskets in the 1920s.

# Fisherman's basketry

The light weight and resistance to corrosion inherent in basketware caused it to be used rather widely by fishermen. Everything from traps to carrying vessels were manufactured in the medium.

## Eel and fish traps

In 1872, Joseph Codding was selling splint eel traps for $1.25 each. These were long double-woven receptacles (see fig. 22), designed so that an eel entering the open end would follow a constricting passageway into a trap area from which it would later be removed by the fisherman. Eels were sought after both for their meat and for their tough skins.

*Figure 22.*

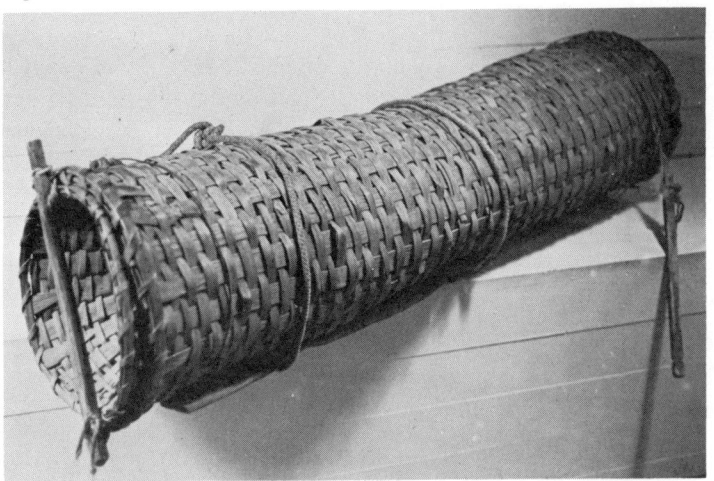

Less common was the fish trap. Shorter and cone-shaped, it was intended for the capture of minnows, small fish used both for food and as bait for larger fish. The principle of construction was identical in both traps.

### Fish, clam, and oyster baskets

The splint fish basket was a commonly seen item on nineteenth-century piers. Similar in shape to a rectangular fruit drying basket but at least a foot high with a stout hickory handle, it was used to unload the catch from arriving boats. The bottom was loosely woven to enable excess water to pass off.

Clam and oyster baskets from quart to bushel were still being made by hand in the early twentieth century. The Pound Ridge basketries were shipping oyster baskets to the fishing fleet at New Haven as late as 1933. The industry had been established in the West Chester County Community in 1841, and by the 1860s oyster baskets commanded a price of $16 per dozen.

### Fishing creels

Freshwater fishermen regularly employ creels, kidney-shaped splint or willow containers carried across the hip on a harness and designed to transport the catch as well as miscellaneous tackle. These have been made for centuries and are made today. Early examples may be distinguished by their construction, generally flatter than present versions, and by the splint or wood trap door in the cover.

### Pack baskets

Sportsmen of all persuasions have recourse to the pack or shoulder basket, an ovoid form with three round sides and a single flat side, which lies flush to the carrier's back. Most pack baskets are made of cross-woven splint, which is light and durable and shapes itself readily to the wearer's shoulders. The term *Indian pack* or *Indian basket* applied to this form reflects its early development by the woodland Indians of North America.

It is generally difficult to date pack baskets; most that are considered antique date from the twentieth century. Daniel Vanavery of Burtonville, New York, was one of the few men to specialize in this line. He made black ash baskets throughout the 1920 and 1930s.

# Willow basketry

Both Indians and settlers used several varieties of willow shrubs and trees as basketry material. Most common was the American green willow, which put out long, smooth branches that were extremely pliable and well suited to weaving. The craftsman would cut these, remove their bark and leaves, and allow them to dry. The branches, or "willow whips," would then be split, or used whole in the smaller sizes. Prepared willow was thoroughly soaked, then woven, generally in the crosshatch pattern characteristic of splint manufacture. The octagon weave was rarely employed.

By 1850, American willow, Welsh or purple willow, and Caspian willow were being cultivated by farmers as a money crop. The plants required five years growth before cutting and were, after 1880, for the most part machine cut and sized.

Owing, perhaps, to limited supply and certainly to its smaller diameter (requiring more material and more weaving to cover the same area), willow was never as widely used as splint, though there can be no doubt as to its antiquity. The estate of Daniel Fisher, of Dedham, Massachusetts, recorded in 1683, listed a "wicker basket," wicker being a common synonym for willowware. In any case, many articles were made of willow and splint in combination, and a substantial number of willow alone.

### Domestic baskets

By the late nineteenth century, basket factories had been established throughout the country, from Maine to California. Their output, in the wicker line, was primarily "fancy ware" intended for use in the home. Much of this was made in standard forms over molds and painted in polychrome colors.

## School, mending, and bonnet baskets

The L. H. Mace and Co. catalog for 1883 listed willow school baskets in several sizes ranging in cost from $2 to 3 per dozen wholesale. These were circular cross-woven containers with a fixed central strap handle and removable covers. They were finished in shellac over the natural tan.

*Figure 23.*

Mending baskets of split willow (fig. 23) were far more common than their splint counterparts. The customary oval form had sides tapering out from the bottom, a flat double cover that enabled the seamstress to open one side at a time, and a fixed central handle similar to that on school baskets. Many of these receptacles were painted with a white ground overlayed by flower sprays in rose, blue, green, or yellow.

Similarly decorated were bonnet or cap baskets in which women going on visits carried their beribboned heargear. A prosaic hood or dust bonnet was worn in transit, and at the end of the journey it was exchanged for the one carried in the basket.

## Clothes baskets and hampers

Nearly half of the willow basketry listed in Mace's 1883 catalog related to the laundry. There were nested oval clothes baskets in small, medium, and large from $6.50 to 9.00 per dozen; square and oval laundry baskets including a set of five "ex. heavy" at $6.50 the dozen; and three sizes of square hampers. All were in a natural finish and were substantially similar to their modern counterparts.

## Flax baskets

Alice Earle, in her *Home Life in Colonial Days*, illustrated a conical openwork flax basket of unsplit willow. This repository for cleaned flax fiber had a circular opening through which the flax was inserted and a shallow loop carrying handle. It was some fourteen inches high by seven in diameter and was left unfinished.

## Utility baskets and boxes

Various utility baskets in willow or willow with splint are the most common items found in this medium. The handled basket shown in figure 24 was probably for storage, while the small open splint and willow containers illustrated in figure 25 are fruit or whatnot baskets.

The large wicker box pictured in figure 26 is the forerunner of today's cat or dog carrier. It dates from the early days of the twentieth century.

*Figure 24.*

FIGURE 25 Above, *whatnot basket;* right, *fruit basket.*

*Figure 26.*

## Cradles

At the death, in 1691, of John Bowles of Roxbury, Massachusetts, the "garretts" of his house were found to contain, among other things, "a wicker cradle." Since no such object appears to have survived the intervening centuries, one may only surmise its shape. However, it might have been similar to the splint cradle previously discussed.

## Farm and market baskets

While most farm containers were of splint or straw, willow was also used. Winnowing fans were often made of splint with willow (also known as osier) bindings. Various field baskets also had similar components.

## Fruit and nut gathering utensils

Several types of wicker fruit-picking containers are known. Their light weight and tight weave made them ideal for this job. The oval basket with bulging sides and large back loop handle illustrated in figure 27 is an excellent example. The loop could be hooked to a belt or carried over the arm, and the footed bottom enabled the vessel to be stood upright when not in use. Another form had double loop handles on the rear edge and was made in the shape of a cylinder eight inches long by six inches in diameter. Still different but serving the same purpose was a flat ovoid split willow receptacle about a foot long and two feet deep, which had a long strap affixed so it could be carried over the shoulder. It fit comfortably under the arm and was probably intended for use in picking apples.

For nut gathering there was an osier receptacle in the shape of a football with an opening in the top just wide enough to insert a handful of nuts. Across this, lengthwise, ran a willow

FIGURE 27 Left to right, *splint sewing basket, willow fruit-picker's basket, splint utility basket.*

strap handle. The clear purpose was to prevent spillage of the contents.

## Market and egg baskets

The ubiquitous market basket, oblong with rigid center strap lift, was also made in wicker. Mace and Co. sold a nest of four in varying sizes from $1.50 to 2.75 per dozen. These were without covers. An "Ex. Fine" covered, braided willow market basket was also sold in four capacities.

An interesting local variation was the so-called Nantucket Basket, which had a board bottom, vertical splints of ash, and fills of willow. The swinging center bail handle was attached to metal ears set into the basket sides. Nests of eight Nantucket baskets from pint to three-gallon size were manufactured in the period 1854–90. They were made primarily by men who worked or had worked on the Nantucket light ship off the Massachusetts coast. Today, they are among the most collectible of baskets.

Willow egg baskets were regularly manufactured throughout the Southern Appalachins. They were ovoid, thus similar in shape to their splint counterparts. One of the better known makers was Aunt Lydia Whaley of Gatlingburg, Tennessee, who wove egg baskets from 1890 to 1925 and taught the craft to a score of others, some of whom still carry on.

## Nesting boxes

Perhaps unique among willowware is the osier chicken nesting box described in Bement's *The American Poulterer's Companion*, which was published in 1867. A rectangular structure with two half-oval doors (opening out into the chicken yard) and corresponding roof hatches for cleaning, it was recommended by Bement "by reason of the constant circulation of air going on through the interstices."

## Pack baskets and fishing creels

The fishing creel and pack basket, though sometimes made of splint, were preferred in willow. Once it dried in shape, osier was stronger than splint and more resistant to moisture, an important aspect with creels. Both items were made with a flat side to fit against the carrier's body and an otherwise ovoid form tapering toward the top, which was wide enough to accommodate entry of various objects.

# Straw basketry

The Palatine Germans who settled parts of New York, New Jersey, and Pennsylvania in the eighteenth century employed straw, primarily rye, in the manufacture of various basket types. The raw material was cut with a hand sickle so that it would be long and unbroken, then fashioned into thick spiral twists. These were then coiled in basket shapes, usually oval or circular, and bound together with narrow strips of heavy cord or hickory bark. Straw baskets were generally undecorated but on occasion might be painted red, green, or blue. As a type, this basketry was termed *Shtrow-Karab* by the Palatines, or Pennsylvania Dutch as they are more familiarly known. Examples are found throughout Pennsylvania, New Jersey, Ohio and Virginia, where straw bread baskets were being made in the 1930s.

## Straw household baskets

Many items that in other areas were manufactured from splint or willow were composed of straw in the Palatine areas. Roofs were thatched with this substance until the 1840s, and straw basketry lingered until the end of the century.

## Breadbaskets

Most common among rye straw containers are breadbaskets, shallow round or oval forms in which freshly kneaded dough was set to rise prior to baking. The piece shown in figure 28 is representative. A loaf of bread would be formed in the basket, wrapped in cloth and set aside to rise. Once the yeast had done its work, the loaf would be baked in an outside or interior

*Figure 28.*

fireplace oven. Some oval breadbaskets were over two feet long, though the majority were much smaller. Handles are common, particularly on larger specimens. For many years it was customary for Palatine children to place breadbaskets rather than stockings at the family fireplace to await Santa Claus's visit.

### Church offering plate

An interesting adaptation of the breadbasket is seen in the rare church offering plate made by simply affixing a four-foot rough wooden handle to the round container. The symbolism involved in use of such a piece surely did not pass unnoticed by the congregation.

### Fruit-drying baskets and trays

The Pennsylvania Dutch used straw to manufacture shallow fruit-drying baskets similar to those made of splint in other sections of the country. They also produced flat trays of this same material, which were used either for drying as or hot plates at the family table.

## Cradles

A basket-shaped cradle of straw is also known, though this form must be considered quite rare. References to a "straw bed" appear in the inventories of several early New Englanders, including that of Ephriam Hewet, who died at Hingham, Massachusetts, in 1678. It is possible, of course, that such beds were really mattresses. A straw cradle, like its splint counterpart, would have had the advantages of light weight and easy portability.

## Carriage wheel shields

Perhaps, the most unusual basketware form of all was the elongated curved straw shield that was used to protect women's long dresses from mud as they got into and out of horsedrawn coaches. Only one of these devices, shaped like a razor clam with a low rim along the back, is known. It is presently at the Henry Ford Museum.

# Farm baskets

### Sower's baskets

A grain sower's basket in straw was used in Pennsylvania. Shaped like a large bread basket, it had two small belt loops on one side and a carrying lift on the other. The farmer would attach it to his waist and support the outer edge by gripping the lift. Then with his free hand he could broadcast the seed.

### Beehives

In 1803, James Humphreys, in his *Gleanings From the Most Celebrated Books on Husbandry*, described "a straw hive consisting of two cylinders, separated from each other by lattices for collecting the honey without destroying the bees." A hive in

*Figure 29.*

this form was listed in a 1683, Suffolk County, Massachusetts, inventory and, until replaced by wood and glass hives in the 1850s, it was the type usually used.

The cone-shaped hive, or bee skep as it was known in Palatine areas, illustrated in figure 29, is typical. It has a small access door on one side, while bees enter a hole at the peak of the cone. When popular, these structures were recommended as being cheaper, warmer in cold weather, and cooler in hot weather than their board or osier counterparts. They are often found still crusted with an ash and dung mixture used to keep unwanted insects from entering the hive.

## Storage hampers

Dried fruit, placed in cotton or linen bags, and grain were often stored in massive lidded straw storage hampers. All of these were somewhat ovoid in shape, and many had such a pronounced "waist" as to be as large around as they were high; often three to four feet. These containers or a stout-handled variation were used to haul freshly picked grapes from the fields. They were also employed as clothes hampers.

## Egg baskets

Egg baskets with narrow necks and flaring bottoms were also made of straw. They were used about the farm for storage and were intended specifically for transporting the large quantities of eggs to market.

# Miscellaneous basketry materials

**Sweet grass**

Along the Atlantic Coast and through the Great Lakes area striped marsh grass known as "sweet grass" was used to some extent, particularly by the Indians, in the manufacture of small utility baskets. The technique generally employed was twining, wherein two or more horizontal wefts were twined around each other as they were woven into the vertical warps.

The grass was gathered in July or August in swampy areas. The whole plant was pulled up and allowed to dry thoroughly. After the roots were removed, the individual leaves of grass were woven into fine strands, which were in turn used to make the containers. Since these strands were very flexible, the basket produced was soft and pliable but quite unsuited to any rough usage. A typical form made was the cap or bonnet basket for carrying fancy ladies' head coverings.

**Pine needles**

During the post-Civil War period a small industry devoted to the manufacture of pine needle baskets grew up in the South, primarily in Tennessee and North Carolina. Needles from the Long Leaf Pine were picked and dried for two or three weeks in the sun until they became brown. Then they were soaked in water to make the needles flexible. After being sewn into long bundles, much the same way straw was prepared, they were woven into a coil bound with cotton thread, raffia, or twine. Stained corn husks or raffia were worked in among the needles to create patterns of color characteristic of this ware.

Many varieties of baskets were thus created, most of them

with covers. The smallest were tiny thimble baskets; the largest, sewing and storage forms a foot or so in diameter. Being quite fragile, all were essentially ornamental in nature.

## Cornshuck

Cornshucks served as ornamental components of various basket forms. They were also used alone in the making of different-sized mats, which might be employed in fruit drying or for placing under hot or wet containers on the dinner table.

## Rattan

Late in the nineteenth century, American basket manufacturers began to import rattan from Southeast Asia as a raw material. A long, tough but flexible palm vine, rattan was cut, dried, and then, stripped of its bark and leaves, cut into suitable lengths. This cutting was originally done by hand, but machines were developed that produced a round or rectangular portion of reed. Both were employed in basketry. The Mace catalog of 1883 listed oval rattan laundry baskets in four sizes from $6.25 to $9.00 per dozen as well as nests of oblong baskets and a special "patent bottom" variety.

At the present time, rattan basketry is far more common than either splint or willow. A wide variety is available, most of it imported from Hong Kong or Taiwan.

## Honeysuckle vine

In areas where honeysuckle is prevalent, the strong pliable vine has been used for weaving tiny ornamental baskets. In the 1930s, Lena Dysart of Rydal, Georgia, who was still working with the material, described its preparation.

We gather the vines from our own farm . . . in winter when the sap is down, wind them in rolls, fasten securely and boil four hours. Remove from pot, run each piece through a cloth to remove bark, soak overnight in a tub of water, rinse in two waters and hang in sunshine to dry. Then, we whittle off each little knot with a sharp pocket knife and then they are ready for weaving.

While most honeysuckle containers are small and ornamental rather than practical, circular, lidded work or sewing baskets are known as well as dry vases and thimble boxes.

# Woodenware

By the seventeenth century, when colonization of this country began, the manufacture of woodenware was a well-recognized trade governed by specific guild regulations and carefully specialized. Any man pursuing the craft was known as a cooper, and there were several classes of these.

Storage vessels were made by "wet" or "dry" coopers, depending on the purpose for which their containers were intended. The former, also known as a "tight" cooper, manufactured large kegs and casks for liquids; his counterpart, the dry, or "slack," cooper, produced barrels for bulk commodities such as flour and sugar.

A third class were the white coopers or dish turners, the men who made the small household treen that is of so much interest to modern collectors. Plates, bowls, tubs, pails, churns, and the like came from their shops.

Finally, two other groups confined themselves wholly to making containers for alcoholic beverages. The butt coopers turned out large barrels and hogsheads for distilleries, while rundlet coopers manufactured swiglers and other small kegs for cordials.

Since every ship was required to carry a cooper to repair water barrels (the well-known John Alden, supposedly, made the trip to Plymouth as a last-minute replacement for an ailing fellow craftsman), a fair number of them must have been among the first settlers. Conditions in the new world made it impossible, however, for the craft to be organized as it had been in Europe. There was a shortage not only of storage vessels but also of the most ordinary table treen. With the demand so great and raw material abundant, every cooper and many noncoopers made every variety of woodenware without regard to specialization.

Flatware (spoons, plates, platters, and shallow bowls) was most readily manufactured because it could be produced without use of a lathe. In the earliest period and, later, in isolated areas, methods similar to those of the Indians were employed. Trees were felled, cut into convenient lengths, and left to dry until properly seasoned for use. The cooper, then, either by gouging alone or by fire-softening and gouging, hollowed out the utensils. Although this work could be done with a knife or even a small axe, the usual tool employed was the cooper's adze, a curved iron blade with a short wooden handle. The arclike design of the adze enabled the craftsman to gouge out and form the interior of the vessel. The exterior was rough cut with an axe, then smoothed down with a two-handed drawknife. This was a long, thin blade with a handle at each end. The cooper would draw it toward himself across the surface to be finished. The jigger, a popular variation, had a blade in part straight, in part curved, so that it could be used on round surfaces such as the outside of bowls.

Completely hand-shaped treen is a prize sought by all collectors. Such vessels may often be recognized by their individuality. No two are ever alike. Often the cutting lines left by a long-deceased craftsman are clearly evident on the surface of a piece. Other treen tends to be of odd shapes, lopsided or unexpectedly oblong. The pieces may often bear signs of crude decoration: incised geometric designs, names, dates, and the like. Burl, an abnormal growth common to certain trees such as the ash, was favored by many early coopers. Its grain, instead of running in the usual parallel lines, was convoluted by disease, which produced an extremely strong texture. Although harder to work, material of this quality was sought for its durability and attractive grain.

For most treen, of course, hand-forming was but a temporary expedient. Crude lathes were soon set up in all areas. Then, as now, the basic purpose of the lathe was to produce a circular movement so that an object fixed on the machine could be cut by chisel-like tools pressed against it. The earliest form was the spring pole lathe, which consisted of a rectangular framework with an attached horizontal arm, which revolved in a socket. This was fastened by cord to a foot treadle and to a curved pole attached to the workshop ceiling. When the foot treadle was depressed, the cord around the work arm unwound, causing it to turn. When the pressure was relaxed the spring of the pole caused the line to rewind. Since this device produced only half a revolution, a bowl or other piece had to be cut or turned in two stages. The mandrel lathe, developed in the seventeenth century, had a continuous action, thus eliminating the need to turn the work to complete both sides.

A wide variety of treen was formed on a lathe. Plates, cups, salts, sugar bowls, and many other utensils were, and still are, manufactured in this manner. Many receptacles, however, were not made from a single solid piece of wood but from several sections that were joined to produce a vessel. There are two general categories of these vessels: boxes and barrels.

Certain containers, such as the dough box, were nailed or dovetailed together in a square or rectangular form. The nails often provide a clue to the age of such receptacles. The earliest, often dating to before 1800, will frequently be joined with handwrought nails recognizable by their hammer-formed heads. After the turn of the century, cut nails, square of head and shank, were employed; and, from about 1880, the familiar wire nail.

Another box form consisted of oval or circular top and bottom plates joined by a flexible strip of veneer wrapped about them. While the board box was really a piece of furniture—in fact, it was often made by cabinetmakers—the veneer container was clearly the province of the cooper. Veneer is simply a strip of thin wood. It is often used in furniture design to give a surface contrast or to cover a common material like pine with a more attractive surface. To be of use in box-making, however, it must be thin and flexible.

The craftsman selected for this work ash or hickory or some other wood that was both flexible and strong. He cut it to approximate shape and shaved it to the desired width. At first this was done by hand with a long, thin-bladed froe that sliced the sections. Later, machinery was devised that could produce a uniform piece of the appropriate depth. In either case, the finished siding sheets were then soaked or steamed until flexible. At the same time, box tops and bottoms of the desired size were cut from thicker slabs of wood, usually pine, after their shapes were marked out with dividers. The veneer siding was wrapped around the top or bottom and nailed or pinned together except in the earliest examples, where it was lapped over and cut to fit without use of external fastenings. All these steps were simple enough to be duplicated by machinery, and after 1850 most boxes were mass-produced in factories.

Barrels, kegs, and buckets differed from boxes in that their sides were made up of many separate narrow pieces of wood rather than a single slab or sheet. The cooper's froe, which was a curved iron blade with a rod handle at a right angle to it, was used to cut these staves. The worker selected a block of wood in the appropriate length and stood it on end. He then hammered the froe down on top of this, slicing off a curved slab corresponding to the shape of the utensil's blade. Each stave slab was then notched at head and foot with a sawlike croze so it could receive the barrel heads. These latter were measured and cut in the same manner as box tops or bottoms. As a next step, the barrel heads were set in and the staves joined together, then bound with hoops to prevent their coming apart. The hoops were made of thin wood, steamed to flexibility, withes, or iron. The mode of construction allowed for expansion and contraction of the contents.

Like boxes, barrels and kegs were primarily factory-made after the middle of the last century. The later items have a uniformity of design and construction that sets them apart from earlier vessels. Mass-production led to a reduction in imaginative design and a decline in the care with which the pieces were made.

Decoration in woodenware is most important. The majority of pieces were either left completely unfinished or, at most, varnished or shellacked. Painting in solid colors or polychrome (red, green, blue, and yellow were most favored) was often employed to finish boxes, storage buckets, and tableware. Incised decoration was generally reserved for more personal belongings such as brides' boxes, pipe racks and goblets. Other things being equal, any decorated example is of more interest than its plain counterpart.

It is extremely difficult to determine the date or place of manufacture of most woodenware. There are a very few pieces that bear an incised date or the manufacturer's name. The most common of the latter are late-nineteenth-century cheese and spice boxes that were stenciled or impressed with the name of the box factory where they were produced. Outside of this minority, the vast bulk of treen can be placed only generally. Certain forms such as salts, noggins, and tankards were, at a relatively early date, replaced by similar vessels in a more satisfactory medium such as ceramics or metal. A mid-nineteenth-century cutoff date can be applied to such items. However, others such as bowls, spoons, and cheese boxes are still being made.

When faced with a problem as to dating or attribution, one must rely heavily on experience; the observation over a period of time of other similar examples. Weight (treen becomes lighter with age), texture, (the smoothness comes from years of handling and washing), wear signs, and patina are all important. But each of these qualities can be faked or may exist naturally on the numerous examples, old but foreign, that have been imported over the years.

Ultimately, collecting woodenware is for the connoisseur of form and the historian of our past culture rather than for the accumulator who requires a group of examples that can be neatly labeled as having been made by a certain craftsman or in a certain locality.

# Wooden cooking ware

Before 1900 a great many utensils and devices considered indispensable to the American home were made of treen. Cooking, baking, and serving all required labor-saving equipment, as did washing, cleaning, and other activities.

The extensive use of fresh bulk food required pioneer families to spend far more time in preparation of meals than is customary today. Everything from spices to meat had to be made ready from a natural state, preserved to the extent possible, and cooked over the uncertain heat of a fireplace or cast iron stove. Of the many utensils required for these various steps, most were wooden, made either on the home farm or in small factories.

### Pothooks, gridirons, and cats

Though the intense heat limited the number of wooden pieces used before the fire, some surviving examples are known. Crudely carved S-shaped pothooks, often taken from a handy tree limb, were used to hang pots above the hearth or in a bake oven. It is seldom possible to date such objects, and their proximity to the flames guaranteed a short life. The majority found today probably served a twentieth-century Boy Scout rather than a nineteenth-century housewife.

There are also a very few early gridirons. These are square or oblong racks made of green wood with high-standing legs and a long handle. They were intended for the broiling of meat or fish over a coal fire and were useful only until the wood dried sufficiently to ignite. The remaining examples invariably show a well-singed undersurface. They were soon replaced by iron grids.

A similar device was the "cat," a trivet formed from three crossed sticks held together by wire or an iron clamp, in the crotch of which a bowl or dish was placed to be heated at the hearth.

## Spatulas and stirrers

Short shovel-shaped pieces of treen, usually maple or another hard wood, were used to turn oatcakes or flapjacks cooking before the fire or atop an old "potbelly" stove. Several examples appear in figure 30. Since these were for the most part hand carved rather than turned, they show a great variation in form.

Stirrers, in several sizes but generally with long handles and flat or round heads had a variety of uses in the kitchen (fig.

FIGURE 30 Above left and right, *butter paddles or workers;* center, *scoops;* below left to right, *dipper, butter paddle, one of a set of Scotch hands, butter spade.*

FIGURE 31 Left to right, 1–4, *spoons and stirrers;* 5–7, *mashers;* 8–9, *rolling pins.*

31). Often the head was pierced with a series of holes or a single rectangular opening to reduce drag while whipping eggs or mixing gruel. Variations in stirrers reflect their intended purpose; the round-topped ones were designed for ovoid batter jugs, and the narrow ones, to fit long-necked jars.

Spatulas and stirrers are made today in both this country and Europe. Since they take on an aged appearance with little use, one must exert care, particularly in purchasing carved ornamental examples.

## Hasty pudding spoons

The preparation of hasty pudding, a gruel made from ground and dried boiled corn, required a special type of stirrer. Since the kettle in which the pudding boiled was placed upon the hearth, a long handle was needed, which was often crooked for better leverage. These implements often show wear at the bowl edge from constant contact with the kettle bottom.

Hasty pudding, also known by the quaint term *gape and swaller* (an apparent allusion to its coarse, gummy quality), was a staple of early settlers' diets, frequently being eaten three times a day.

## Eggbeaters

An interesting variation of the stirrer is the early wooden eggbeater. A small bow with string attached to a stirrer was set into a wooden frame so that moving the bow back and forth would cause the stirrer to turn. The principle was similar to that of the bow drill with which Indians made holes and started fires.

## Toddy and swizzle sticks

Some interesting beverage mixers are often confused with common stirrers and no doubt were at times interchangeable with these. Toddy sticks were turned dowel forms, generally about six to ten inches long, often with a bulbous or spoon-shaped head. They were used to crush the lemon and sugar for a Flip or a Toddy. An example is illustrated in figure 32. Flip was a common fireside drink made from sugar, spices, sherry, and eggs. A Toddy had as ingredients spirits, sugar, lemon, and hot water. Both were hot drinks generally warmed with a poker heated in the fire.

Swizzle, on the other hand, was a mixture of spirits, sugar,

FIGURE 32 Left, *knife box;* above right, *covered box (probably for spice);* center, *spigot;* below, *swizzle stick.*

and bitters; it was laced with ice and served cold. Swizzle sticks were long rods, twelve to fourteen inches in length, with cross arms or a winged head. They were commonly held between the palms and spun rapidly to agitate the drink. The plain whittled shank of the swizzle stick is readily distinguished from the ornate turned toddy stirrer.

## The mortar and pestle

From earliest times, a hollow mortar with a matching rodlike pestle was used to grind spices, grain, or medicinal herbs. The common form was lathe turned, six to ten inches high and

FIGURE 33 Left to right, *covered sugar bowl, mortar and pestle, grain mortar and pestle.*

generally made of a wood such as maple or pine. A few mortars were manufactured of the extremely hard and most attractive lignum vitae. In 1814, the renowned cabinetmaker Nathaniel Dominy V., of East Hampton, Long Island, produced a mortar and pestle in this material for John Gardiner, scion of Gardiner's Island. Another such set, valued at two shillings, eight pence, was in the estate of Ebenezer Dorr, who died at Roxbury, Massachusetts, in 1760.

Mortars were produced in several forms and many sizes, from three-inch miniatures used by physicians to corn grinders over two feet tall. This size range is reflected in the examples shown in figure 33. Those in the normal range were used for a number of purposes. While they may be characterized as spice, snuff, or herb mortars, such designation is often meaningless, since few families could afford a form to suit each function. Pestles found with mortars are seldom original. The original ones wore out or were lost long ago, or, as was often the case, there never was a matching pestle—any blunt object was sufficient to do the job at hand.

## Spice mills and grinders

Spice mills and grinders were related objects. The former are best known as boxlike shapes similar to old coffee mills but somewhat smaller. In this version an iron handle turns interlocking teeth within the box, thus grinding the spice, which is then removed through a drawer. Less common is the boat-shaped mill known in colonial times as the "sow and pigs." This is an ovoid wooden dish or trough with a round-handled blade made of steel or wood, which is rolled back and forth across the trough to pulverize its contents.

Miniature individual spice grinders are also known. They are made in two parts, one fitting into the other and both set with meshing steel teeth. When the top is turned within the bottom, the teeth crush the spices inside.

## Spice bowls and chests

Ground spice for table and kitchen use was often kept in bowls or boxes with close-fitting lids, such as that shown in figure 32. The earlier examples are ovoid; the later ones have straight sides. In each case a well-formed finial graces the cover. The average height is four to six inches. These containers are often confused with sugar bowls, which are similar in form. The odor of spice is often the only clue to original use.

FIGURE 34 Left, *spice cabinet;* upper right, *eating bowls and spoon;* lower right, *plates.*

In the Victorian era a revolving factory-made spice storage chest was introduced. A circular container was divided into pie-shaped compartments each bearing a stenciled label denoting the condiment it contained. The vessel revolved in its frame in the manner of a "Lazy Susan." An example, patented in 1866, is in the Shelburne Museum collection at Shelburne, Vermont. Earlier spice chests were made by cabinetmakers and had compartmented drawers such as those of the one pictured in figure 34.

## Spice canisters

Another factory-produced spice holder was the circular veneer spice canister, about eight inches in diameter, which contained within it eight smaller canisters, each intended for a separate

FIGURE 35 Left to right, *wood veneer spice canister set, sieve, cheese boxes.*

spice (see fig. 35). These receptacles were also individually marked with the name of a spice. Canister sets of this sort are very popular with collectors, and are often marked. The name of the Boston Wooden Box Manufactory often appears on such items.

## Sieves and graters

The rural household also had a selection of round and oval sieves used in refining sugar, salt, spices, and herbs. An example is shown in figure 35. Both sugar and salt were obtained in blocks that had to be crushed and then sifted to a usable consistency. The sieves for this purpose were made from horse mane or tail hair woven into a mat on a small loom. This mat was then clamped between two sturdy oak or ash frames, one of which fit inside the other like embroidery hoops. Marshall Stedman of Tyringham, Massachusetts, made such sieves from 1887 until as late as 1927.

Some sieves had one or two fitted wooden covers to protect the mat and to catch the siftings. Hair was later replaced as a material by tin or brass wire (brass was favored by Shaker craftsmen), and white silk "bolting cloth." L.H. Mace and Co.,

FIGURE 36  Left, *apple parer;* right, *sugar and flour sifter.*

FIGURE 37 Above left, *eating bowl;* back center, *pie peel;* front center, *sausage gun;* right, *grater;* below left, *fingered herb boxes;* right, *apple-drying tray.*

woodenware manufacturers of New York City, sold nests of three "plated Wire" sifters for $1.25 per dozen in the 1880s. Each of the three sieves was of a different size.

A box sifter was also common in the nineteenth century. This was a rectangular wooden receptacle with a wire bottom and revolving wood or tin paddles that were moved by turning an exterior crank. Such devices were used to refine large quantities of flour and sugar. The form shown in figure 36 (right) is typical.

Another familiar item was the grater, generally a square or oblong frame into which was nailed a piece of punched tin. While many graters, particularly after 1850, were factory-made, a large number of unusual forms are known. An oblong chopping bowl had its worn bottom replaced with pierced metal. A solid slab of wood with a circular orifice was similarly treated. Another crude but servicable type is pictured in figure 37. While not as common as later all-metal forms, treen graters are frequently found in shops and at flea markets. Some of these may be of great age. An example in the Gould collection was dated "1740."

## Vegetable slicers

Somewhat related is the vegetable slicer. This was composed of a rectangular piece of wood with a semicircular opening into which was set a sharp blade. Carrots, potatoes, and the like were scraped across the cutting edge and reduced to slivers. Similar slicers are available in modern stores, and older examples are generally factory products no more than a hundred years old, such as the one illustrated in figure 38.

Box-like footed vegetable cutters, such as the one seen in figure 39, were also employed. They had an interior rather than exterior blade.

FIGURE 38  Back center, *vegetable slicer;* right, *meat pounder;* center, *lard squeezers;* below left, *lemon squeezer.*

FIGURE 39  Left, *meat grinder;* right, *vegetable slicer.*

## Meat pounders, grinders, and masticators

Lacking artificial tenderizers, colonial housewifes resorted to a variety of methods to prepare meat for the table. Most common was the pounder, or steak maul, a shape familiar to contemporary chefs. The Mace catalog of 1883 offered these with corrugated heads and long handles. They came in two sizes; the smaller at ninety cents per dozen, the larger at a dollar a dozen. A less common variant had a pyramid-shaped head tapering toward the short handle, and a third type was in the form of a wooden hammer with sharp teeth cut into the face. All were manufactured from maple or an equally hard wood.

For one who wanted to concoct a form of pre-twentieth-century hamburger, there was the masticator, a wooden-handled board with rows of flat iron teeth set into one side. Dating from the 1880s, the masticator was used to shred meat that was rubbed over its coarse surface. Another form, illustrated in figure 38, had a short handle and was used to beat and tear the flesh.

Somewhat more sophisticated is a meat grinder in the Farmers' Museum collection at Cooperstown, New York, which is shown at figure 39. It consists of a set of wooden pegs seated on a roller in a spiral pattern so that they pass between parallel lines of sharp tin blades. The apparatus is housed in a wooden box, into the sides of which the blades are fixed. The receptacle has a lift top through which the meat is inserted to be dragged across the cutting edges as the roller is turned by a crank. David Evans of Philadelphia, though better known for his furniture, manufactured such devices in the late eighteenth century.

### Powdering tubs, lard squeezers, and sausage stuffers

Meat preservation was a serious problem in pre-electrical America. Ice was available only in certain sections of the country; and drying, a method popular with the Indians, produced an unattractive, unpalatable dish. Accordingly, decay-resistant spices were used as a preservative. "Powdering tubs" such as that listed in the 1755 estate inventory of Samuel Pratt at Chelsea, Massachusetts, were used in salting or "powdering" fresh meat. These vessels were made of staves in the manner of a barrel and ranged up to three feet in diameter. Their tops were smaller than their bottoms with a noticeable upward taper.

Alternating layers of meat and rock salt were laid in these tubs and left until the condiment had impregnated the flesh. The process didn't always work. Miriam Rawson, in her *Handwrought Ancestors*, records an old farmer as noting of powdering tubs, that "when the meat spoiled in it, you better throw the whole thing right out, it's no use any more."

Pork was preserved in the form of a highly spiced sausage. Different kinds of sausage stuffers were utilized in forcing the ground meat into skin casings. A typical one was a tin tube with wooden plunger (see fig. 37). The sausage mixture was packed into this tube, then ejected into the skin, which was attached to the funnel-shaped tube mouth, by depressing the plunger. A larger early butchers' version was set into a wooden bench and operated like a well pump.

Hog fat was used to manufacture cooking lard, which did not deteriorate readily. After being cooked, the fat was tied in a bag and compressed in a lard squeezer. This was composed of two flat wooden sticks attached at one end by a leather strap or metal hinge. A commercially manufactured example is illustrated in figure 38. Under pressure, the lard ran off and was caught in a container for storage. Squeezers in this form were also used to crack lobster shells. Two more complex lard squeezers are shown in figure 60. These are much less common than the usual form.

## Bowls

"Wooden boles" were listed among the possessions of Benjamin Childe when he died at Roxbury, Massachusetts, in 1678. Nearly two hundred years later Mace and Co. was advertising similar vessels in nests of seven from eleven to twenty-four inches in diameter.

In the intervening period a great number of these receptacles were formed either by hand carving or turning. The first were made by charring the center of a wooden block to soften the wood, which was then roughed out with an axe and drawknife. The exterior was treated in a similar manner. Most of the existing specimens belong to a later period and were turned on a lathe.

In either case, with the passage of time, the circular bowl warps to an ovoid, often splitting in the process. The value once placed on these vessels is reflected in the number of existing ones that bear brass or iron repairs to such age cracks.

Most bowls were round, though some were oval and a very few hexagonal or even square. They were made primarily from maple, pine, or birch, with choice examples in burl, and ranged in size from a few inches to three feet in diameter.

FIGURE 40  Back, *butter bowl and butter worker;* below left to right, *butter spade and keeler, butter packing tamp, one-pound butter mold.*

Form varied to suit the use intended. Milk and grease bowls were shallow; the former were straight-sided, the latter had rounded lips. Similar in shape to the grease bowl was the cheese drainer bowl, a vessel with holes drilled in its base to allow liquid to pass off. Cheesecloth attached to wooden pegs covered the base of this receptacle. Butter bowls or trays and bread-making bowls were generally deeper and larger than the above.

However, householders used these containers interchangeably. Often the only way their prime function may be determined is by examination of residue. Grease bowls show a dark oily stain; milk bowls are bleached white; butter bowls (see

FIGURE 41  Left to right, *soft-soap scoop, platter, chopping bowl.*

Wooden cooking ware 71

fig. 40) have a distinct fat line; and bread bowls bear a dry white tinge. All may eventually serve as chopping bowls where the abrasive action of the iron blade soon works through the base of the vessel. A chopping bowl or oblong chopping tray, (see fig. 41), is readily recognized by the interlacing scratches covering the lower interior. In the late nineteenth century, certain bowls were factory made, specifically for chopping. The example shown in figure 42 was termed a chopette and made in Rochester, New York.

Bowls, particularly the uncommon examples in burl or lignum vitae or those that are hand-shaped, are among the most collectible of woodenware. They are occasionally found painted white or blue, but the majority have been left in a natural state.

FIGURE 42 Above left to right, *fisherman's line winder, chopping bowl, cribbage board;* below left and right, *yarn winders.*

## Mashers and chopping boards

Among the more expendable kitchen items were turned wooden mashers and chopping boards. Mashers, which may be distinguished from steak mauls by their flat heads and lack of corrugations, were made of pine or maple. Mace and Co. sold them by the dozen for as little as sixty-five cents. They occasionally have interesting, turned shafts but are generally common and undistinguished. Several examples appear in figure 31.

Although chopping boards were sold commercially (Mace and Co. offered them in ash as "meat boards"), most were fashioned at home from a handy slab of wood. They were soon cut to pieces and replaced. Accordingly, few found are of any age and fewer still are well shaped, though often the worn, grease-impregnated wood has an attractive aged appearance, as may be seen from figure 43.

*Figure 43.*

## Lemon squeezers

Lemons, whose juice was an important ingredient of early beverages, were squeezed in several different devices. Most simple was a turned handle with corrugated head, which was ground into the hand-held lemon half. More common were two-piece hinged squeezers. These were similar in form to a lard squeezer but with a depression on one side to hold the lemon and a corresponding protuberance on the opposite wing. The lemon was split in two and each half pressed by contracting the pincers. This form was illustrated in the 1883 Mace catalog and is shown in figure 38. Two sizes were available. The smaller sold for $1.00 per dozen, the larger cost $1.25 for the same quantity.

Another variation was a small table mounted on legs with a handle, which, upon being depressed, squeezed the lemon half. The motion used was similar to that utilized in pumping water from a well. The juice ran off the surface through a shallow trough and was collected in a glass or bowl.

## Sauerkraut stompers

Stamping rather than squeezing was employed in making sauerkraut, a salted shredded cabbage that was fermented in its own juice. The sauerkraut stomper, which was a long stick with a heavy plungerlike head, was used to compress the vegetable mass as it aged.

## Apple parers and slicers

Fruit and vegetable preparation required enough time in the colonial home to justify labor-saving devices, and many are known. Apple parers were made in the United States as early as 1750, and the first patent for such a device was issued in 1803 to Moses Coates of Downing Fields, Pennsylvania. This

FIGURE 44  Left, *cherry pitter;* right, *apple slicer.*

was a wooden machine consisting of a large wheel with ratchets, which engaged another smaller wheel upon which was affixed an iron fork. The apple was placed on the fork and peeled by being rotated against a fixed knife blade. While treen parers were not completely replaced by metal versions until the mid-nineteenth century, relatively few remain. A Delaware example in oak is illustrated in the Index of American Design, and another is at the Huntington, New York, Historical Society. The example shown in figure 36 (left) is from the collection of the Farmers' Museum in Cooperstown, New York.

Apple slicers are a later innovation, and quite a few find their way into shops. Wooden versions consist of a box with inset blade or blades against which apples are pressed either by hand or mechanical means. The circular slicer, illustrated in figure 44, is a particularly fine example.

## Cherry pitters and raisin seeders

The wooden cherry seeder also took several forms. Most often seen is one resembling the "one arm bandit" or table top slot machine pictured in figure 44. The seeder has a well-formed base and vase-shaped body topped by a traylike surface containing holes through which cherries are inserted. An attached arm is affixed to interior picks in such a way that pulling back on the arm causes the picks to gouge out the pits as cherries pass through the machine.

Far less complex is a crude raisin seeder produced by anchoring a set of wires in a wooden handle. This tool was raked back and forth in a bowl of raisins until the seeds worked out of the pulpy mass and through the wire.

## Ice cream freezers

Stave-constructed, tinbound buckets in which ice cream was frozen were a popular Victorian item, and many are still in use. The containers had a capacity of from two to twenty-five quarts, and came with an iron crank and paddles to turn the ice mixture. Mace and Co. offered a double-action type and side crank models as well as the "Celebrated Triple Motion White Mountain Freezer," which cost from $3.75 to $25.00 depending upon capacity.

## Funnels and spigots

Funnels of various sizes graced the early kitchen. They were primarily of lathe-turned maple or birch and were factory-made after 1850. Most examples were less than six inches long.

There were also wooden spigots or faucets for use in water coolers and beer kegs. These varied in length from six to seventeen inches and were usually turned, as is the one shown in figure 32. Similar items are made today, and it is often difficult to determine if a particular example is of any age.

## Salt-boxes

Every kitchen also had its salt-box, a square or semiround box with hinged cover, which stood on a table or, more often, hung from the wall. Most examples were about six by eight inches. Early boxes, particularly from Pennsylvania, may be scratch-carved in great detail, with geometric designs prevailing. Such containers have been reproduced, but later models may be recognized by the use of wire nails and a general sloppiness in construction never found in nineteenth-century salt-boxes. And, of course, the form goes back to the earliest settlers. William Savery of Philadelphia was making them in the 1770s.

# Baking utensils

Breadstuffs, from corn, rye, or wheat, were the main element in the pioneer diet. In the earliest days, these were baked in hot ashes before the fire. Later, ovens located either at the back or side of the fireplace, or as in Pennsylvania, entirely outside the house, served the purpose more efficiently. The baking process varied from one area to another, but certain utensils were always necessary.

### The bannock board

Perhaps the earliest American baking device was the bannock board, used to bake cornmeal cakes on the hearth. This was a wooden slab a foot long and half as wide with a protruding handle on one side that also served to prop the board up at an angle. The cakes were placed on the opposite side from this handle and cooked in the direct heat of the fire.

### Flour scoops and sifters

In those areas where the grain could be cultivated, wheat flour was soon used in baking. It was stored in barrels and removed with a shell-shaped handleless scoop. Sifting was at first done with the hair or wire hand sifter, previously described, but by the mid-nineteenth century factory-made versions had been developed. These were box-shaped, set on legs, with a wooden arm that moved back and forth when cranked to sift the grain down through a wire screen. A similar device was used in sugar sifting. An example may be seen in figure 36.

## Bread troughs, boards, and knives

Bread was made from wheat flour either in a turned bread bowl or, more often, in a bread trough or tray like the one shown in figure 45. This latter was originally a hollowed log with cover, later a rectangular board box with sides tapering out from the bottom and dovetailed corners. The trough might also have a hole at each end into which fit a rod that supported a tin flour sieve. The addition of turned legs made the bread trough into a piece of furniture.

FIGURE 45 Left, *covered dough box;* right, *keeler and butter tamp.*

As early as 1695, the estate inventory of Joseph Wise, a resident of Roxbury, Massachusetts, listed a "kneeding trough"; and, in 1776 a similar piece owned by William Vassall was termed a "bread trough."

Bread was kneaded or rolled out on the bread trough lid or on a round or rectangular bread board with batten ends. The rectangular one was sometimes decorated with an edging of impressed fruit or flower motifs. An extremely fine specimen from Louisiana commemorated the battle of New Orleans with an embossed bust of Andrew Jackson and the words New Orleans, July 8.

Knife-shaped wooden shafts, some over two feet long, were used to cut the dough into loaves or other suitable shapes. These dough knives are seldom seen today, though troughs and boards remain common.

## Rolling pins

In 1775, William Savery, the well-known Philadelphia cabinetmaker, listed among his accounts a man named James Pemberton, for whom he made a rolling pin. Though it cannot be ascertained, this was probably the early handleless version. Later rollers had one and finally two handles as in the modern type. Both stationary and revolving handle varieties were offered by Mace in 1883, the latter costing twenty-five cents more per dozen.

Most rolling pins were of maple, though some were mahogany, lignum vitae, and cherry. Sizes varied from three-inch children's models to giant three-foot bakers' rollers. Those with corrugated grooves rather than a smooth surface were intended as cookie rollers. The rarest version is one or two rollers set in a frame and known, appropriately enough, as a "wringer type" roller. This form and a simple handled variety are shown in figure 31.

## Cookie and gingerbread prints / Springerle boards

Flat circular discs with a design (bird, flower, star, etc.) cut into one or both sides and bearing no evidence of having had a handle are cookie prints that were used to stamp a pattern

FIGURE 46   Left to right, *gingerbread print, mousetrap, bee-finder's box.*

into a tray of cookie dough. They should not be confused with butter prints, which always have handles.

Gingerbread prints are oblong wooden blocks divided into sections each of which has a design. In some such prints all sections will have the same motif; in others, the characterization will vary from square to square with rabbits, squirrels, and a variety of flowers appearing on the same board. An example is pictured in figure 46.

While cookie prints were a product of Pennsylvania and New York, gingerbread stamps appear throughout the North Atlantic states.

In Pennsylvania print carving was carried to a high point in the Springerle board, which was used for baking Easter cakes. These stamps varied from one or two through a dozen cupcakelike sections, each of which was intricately cut in geometric patterns, the so-called Frisian carving. The design was in intaglio so that, pressed into cake dough, the stamps produced patterns in bas-relief.

Known simply as cake boards in other areas, these molds could also be used by forcing soft dough into the individual forms. One of these, which was once in the collection of the Ohio Historical Society, was marked W. I. and was made for an Ashland County, Ohio, family around 1840.

## Marzipan molds

Individual molds cut in the same manner and varying from two to eight inches at widest point were used to form marzipan candy. Marzipan consisted of ground almond paste or fine cornmeal laced with honey. Forced into the mold, the paste hardened into a block of candy imprinted with a crown, leaf, or similar motif.

Well-cut cake, gingerbread, or marzipan molds are much sought after by today's collectors. Unfortunately, modern reproductions and European imports make it extremely difficult to determine the authenticity of a given piece.

## Doughnut cutters and pie crimpers

Other baked goods required different utensils. Doughnuts were shaped with a cutter, usually of tin and rarely of wood. The edges of a piecrust were pinched together with wooden pie crimpers, circular-toothed wheels that revolved on a handled frame. Some crimpers had shapely lathe-turned handles and bone wheels. They were also used to cut apart cookie sheets.

## Bread and pie peels, pielifters

Goods to be baked were placed in the hot oven by means of several devices. The bread peel, a long-handled, flat-headed wooden shovel often five feet in length, was used to slide loaves of bread into and out of the beehive ovens. Three examples appear in figure 47. It was believed to be a good omen to present a bride with one of these lifts. The few remaining examples usually show a thin, worn edge owing to contact with the oven floor.

Pie peels had a wider head and much shorter handles (see fig. 37). They served to transfer pies to and from the ovens. A more modern device, the pie lifter, was simply a short wooden handle with two wire extensions, one of which fit on

FIGURE 47  *Bread peels.*

each side of the pie plate. Pie peels are the older form. One was made for Philadelphian Daniel Trotter by the cabinet-maker John Downes in 1789.

## Pie boxes

The pie, after baking, was often stored or carried in a pie box, which was a circular covered container with an interior tray on legs. One pie was placed in the bottom of the box, the second on the tray above it. These receptacles resemble a cheese box but are much more scarce.

# Tableware

Because of severe space limitations aboard the early ships, little ceramic, glass, pewter, or silver tableware was brought to the New World prior to 1700. Even thereafter, these materials were in short supply on the frontier. The settlers found Indians eating from wooden bowls and quickly adopted the custom. As a result, farm tables were for many years partially or completely set with this ware.

## Bowls

Eating bowls in a variety of forms and materials are among the more common woodenware. Examples appear in figures 34 and 37. Hamilton Fairchild of Jeffersonville, Indiana, furnished a good part of his state with turned ash bowls during the 1850s and 1860s. Many other men worked in the field as well. Some of their receptacles were shallow; others were deeper, like modern salad bowls. Maple, pine, and chestnut were popular raw materials; and the pieces were at first laboriously hand carved. The few remaining early specimens have rolled edges and ornamental grooving on the exterior. Later machine-made bowls have little or no lip and smooth outer surfaces.

Burl bowls are among the most choice. An extremely rare form is the footed burl fruit bowl shown in Card's *The Use of Burl in America*. Ornamental ridging and a well-turned foot make it clear that this was intended to be a decorative piece.

## Porringers

An archaic bowl form is the porringer, a shallow round container with one or two handles. Wooden porringers are similar to the more common silver and pewter examples and, like these, were used to hold porridge, gruel, and other soft foods. Some porringers have flat handles typical of the metal varieties. Others have a round, curved holder such as that on a dipper.

## Plates or trenchers

Plates were at least as common as eating bowls in the colonial home. The 1691 inventory of Jonathan Avery at Dedham, Massachusetts, listed "two duson of Trenchers," while "woodenware plates" were among the possessions of Ebenezer Jones of Dorchester when they were cataloged in 1735. The term *trencher*, from an ancient French word meaning to cut or carve, was in common use here until the 1800s.

The earliest examples are square, with a depressed circular area in which the food was placed. There is often a second and smaller cavity in one corner for salt. An American trencher of this sort is in the Sturbridge Museum collection, but most were brought here from Europe. More often seen are the round, flat dishes with a broad rim once known as lossets. Two appear in figure 34.

Plates generally are from five to fourteen inches in diameter and three or four inches deep. They were once so scarce that two people ate from the same one. When the diners were of the opposite sex and unmarried, the act was taken to signify a plighting of troth.

Even after pewter and pottery replaced them, wooden trenchers had a role. The story is told of a nineteenth-century husbandman who fed his aged father from wooden dishes for fear that the palsied gentleman would break anything less durable. Finding his own young son whittling away one day, the master of the house asked what was being made. "A wooden plate, sir," replied the youth. "And for what use," asked his father. "To feed you on when you are old," was the quick response.

## Platters and trays

Treen platters were of two shapes, oval and oblong. The former, called chargers, were often eighteen inches in diameter. The latter (an example of which appears in fig. 41), were sometimes even larger. Mary Earle Gould owned a pine pig platter three feet long. It was intended to accommodate an entire suckling pig including apple! These oblong or rectangular vessels were also termed salvers. One appears under that name in the estate of Joseph Gooch, who died at Milton, Massachusetts, in 1770.

The form was most popular in New York and Pennsylvania, although it is known elsewhere. Jonathan Avery of Dedham, Massachusetts, had one in his seventeenth-century home, and another was made for John Gardiner by Nathaniel Dominy IV of East Hampton, Long Island. Maple, ash, and pine were preferred woods.

With the passage of time, chargers came to be referred to as trays. The Mace catalog listed four sizes in 1883, from seventeen to twenty-five inches in diameter. Even the largest cost less than fifty cents apiece.

The Shakers manufactured a rectangular tray with two-inch sides, which was used in apple drying or as a table tray. It was frequently painted in the shade known as Shaker Red.

## Mugs, tankards, and noggins

Squat, handled wooden mugs were a common sight in early country homes and taverns. They were either turned from a single block of wood with a whittled handle added or were made of staves with a solid bottom, the handle being carved integral with one of the staves. Hoops of iron or thin hickory were bound about the mugs to hold the staves in place. Joseph Webster of Weare, New Hampshire, was making these mugs in the mid-nineteenth century.

Tankards are similar but taller and always have a cover

FIGURE 48  Left to right, *ladle with turned bowl, noggin, staved tankard.*

affixed to the top of the handle stave by a wooden or iron pin. They too are staved and hooped. Samples are shown in figures 48 and 49. Toddy, the communal drink, was served in tankards, some of which have a hole in the cover through which a hot iron was thrust to heat the drink. Tankards generally are made of pine, and some of them are found painted in red or black.

Early pitchers were called noggins. They had pouring lips but no covers and were, in most cases, turned from a single piece of wood. Occasionally, eight- or ten-sided carved specimens appear. Sizes of up to four cups are known. They were used both as pitchers and as drinking vessels. A well-shaped pitcher is illustrated in figure 48.

FIGURE 49  Left and center, *storage buckets for flour or sugar;* right *staved tankard.*

## Cups, goblets, and glasses

True loophandled cups are rare in wood. More common is a deep bowl-shaped vessel with a short, curved handle. This can be classified either as cup or porringer and no doubt served the purpose of each.

Footed goblets are an old form clearly patterned on silver prototypes. George Lehn, a retired Lancaster, Pennsylvania, farmer, established a reputation in the late nineteenth century with his decorated goblets and egg cups. He favored red, green, and white floral patterns on a dull pink or yellow background. In other areas the goblet was less ornate, as may be observed from the example in figure 43.

Straight-sided glasses were easy to make on a lathe, and a substantial number, many of them novelty or souvenir items, exist as remnants of the Victorian era.

## Bottles and bottle corkers

Treen bottles were probably never common. There were two in the estate of John Farrington of Dedham, Massachusetts, valued in 1676 at one shilling, sixpence for the pair, a substantial sum at the time. The few existing examples are turned and clearly intended to duplicate glass bottles of the period.

Collectors will have little trouble acquiring a wooden bottle corker. This is a two-piece apparatus with a plunger, which, when depressed, caused a cork to be compressed and forced into the neck of a wine bottle. They are made today.

## Spoons, ladles, and spoon holders

Wooden spoons are a common item in antique shops, but those offered are seldom of any age. Their fragility and commonplaceness guaranteed an early demise, and few unusual pieces are to be found. Yet, they are still manufactured; and, in fact, spoons of laurel were once so common in Pennsylvania that the tree was known as "spoonwood." Early forms with blunt handle and thick bowl (fig. 34), the Scottish porridge spoon, or "Brose Spoon," were followed by long-handled cooking and stirring spoons such as those seen in figure 31. The 1883 Mace catalog offered five varieties: "soft wood," "turned," "Day's" (a patent item), mustard, and salad spoons, the latter of boxwood. A hundred years previous, the turner Thomas Clark of Wrentham, Massachusetts, advertised "spoons," nothing more.

Ladles for table and kitchen use have always been available. They are listed in early inventories, and were offered in two sizes by Mace, at ninety cents and one dollar per dozen. They are larger and more likely to be decorated than spoons. An interesting homemade form appears in figure 48.

Decoration, usually cut or raised, in these utensils is rare and of course most desirable. However, it should be noted that much incised spoonware is now being imported from southern Europe.

Spoons and ladles at the table were often kept in a plain turned spoon holder shaped like a water tumbler. A less common form was of hollow poplar with a pegged-in bottom.

## Forks

The Sturbridge collection contains several early wooden forks. They have three sharpened tines and a finial-tipped handle. This was the seventeenth-century form. In the succeeding century, a fourth tine was added, and the finial became a blunt terminus. Today the cycle is complete with the three-tined salad fork (an item also offered by Mace), a common barbecue tool.

## Butter knives and dishes

Long, thin butter knives, generally a turned handle with shaved blade, were used in conjunction with butter dishes. The latter were turned circular plates similar to eating dishes but bearing around the shoulder in raised letters the word *Butter*. They are of a later period, dating primarily from the Victorian era.

### Knife trays

Knife trays (open, two-part wooden boxes) such as the one appearing in figure 32, were used for many years to store table knives. They were placed on the table in these containers and returned to them after the meal dishes had been washed. As a result, a knife box of any age bears knife scars on the interior and sides.

Most were made of pine, poplar, or walnut. A few had hinged or sliding lids, and fewer still were decorated. An exceptional example from Pennsylvania dating to 1810 has a divider carved in the shape of two doves and a heart. It is polychrome, but most such containers were colored red, blue, black, or another single hue.

The finest specimens were produced in the northeast; Isaac Ashton of Philadelphia made mahogany knife trays; and Nathaniel Dominy of Long Island, in 1807, furnished an example in cherry to his neighbor, Jeremiah Miller. L.H. Mace and Co. made two styles: flared sides in pine and walnut and straight-sided in stripes (matched light and dark wood).

### Sugar bowls

Sugar bowls, for the earlier brown and later commercial white sugar, were a common table vessel. The earliest (fig. 33) were in a bulbous form, similar to the "turnip" foot of seventeenth-century case furniture. Nineteenth-century examples favored a barrel or even a straight-sided shape. In either case a well-turned top with finial was fitted tightly to the vessel.

Varying in diameter from four to fifteen inches and made in a variety of hardwoods, sugar bowls (or boxes, as they were earlier called) are among the most attractive of treen.

Philadelphian William Savery was making them before 1800, and Hiram Pease of Lake County, Ohio, made thousands between 1850 and 1900.

## Urns

Very similar to sugar bowls are decorated lathe-turned urns, which were utilized by the Pennsylvania Dutch for spice containers. They are distinguished by a foot or stem in contrast to sugar bowl, which sat flush upon the table. They too have domed covers with finials and may be recognized by the lingering odor of a long-used spice. Urns are often decorated with punched or incised motifs—geometrics, flowers, etc.—as opposed to the rarely ornamented sugar bowls. An interesting example illustrated in the *Index of American Design* has the usual painted cornucopias and tulips plus a swag and tassel motif about the rim, which clearly reflects the influence of English style on a rural Germanic culture.

## Salts

Another, generally footed utensil is the salt. Initially a single salt container served an entire table with social rank being expressed in terms of who sat "above" or "below" the salt. Long before the first settlers came to this continent, the custom had been modified to allow for a single "master" salt (sometimes six inches in diameter) and various individual salts, two or three inches across, which were filled from the master as required.

While a few covered salts are recorded, most had no tops. They were usually circular and bowl-shaped, but straight-sided (see fig. 50) and even rectangular forms are known. As in sugar bowls, burl was a popular medium. More often, though, a hard, clear wood such as maple was favored. Glistening salt crystals readily distinguish the salt from similarly shaped sugar bowls and urns.

FIGURE 50    Above, *checkerboard (men are made of sliced corncob);* below left to right, *turned salt, ink sander, turned inkwell.*

## Egg cups

A late-nineteenth-century innovation was the turned egg cup, which in contrast to modern glass or ceramic examples had a large flared base and bowl, often decorated with painted floral patterns over a solid yellow or pink background. George Lehn, of Lancaster, Pennsylvania, made a number of these that have survived to grace the collection of the Landis Valley Museum, at Landis Valley, Pennsylvania.

## Napkin rings and table mats

Wooden napkin rings or serviettes, both plain and decorated, appeared in the mid-nineteenth century. They were turned on a lathe and frequently had one or more incised lines running about the center. Decorative coloration was uncommon, with most rings being of stained walnut or maple.

Like napkin rings, table mats were essentially a luxury item. It is doubtful that any existed in the eighteenth century, and wicker or cornshuck "made do" for most of the nineteenth. However, by 1883, L.H. Mace and Co. could provide an ovoid set of six "made of alternate strips of light and dark wood, polished, fastened securely to cloth, thus making them flexible, and finished in a fine manner."

## Toothpick holders

Another late form was the toothpick holder, a barrel-shaped receptacle with a stem and a wide-turned foot. The Ohio turner Hiram Pease often made these with a decorative loose ring circling the stem, and lines of blue about the body. The form is still being manufactured.

## Punch bowls and syrup jugs

A rare and early shape is the treen punch bowl. Most of the existent examples date to the eighteenth century. They were large, often a foot in diameter, with a massive base. Maple or ash were the usual woods, and the finest examples were hewn rather than turned. Such bowls were replicas of silver pieces and much less common.

Another unusual form is the syrup jug, a narrow staved and hooped vessel. This differs from the tankard only in that a tiny pouring spout is fashioned from the stave directly opposite the handle. Such a jug is in the Gould collection, but I know of no others.

## Cheese planes

Colonial ingenuity is reflected in a unique plane that was used to slice cheese at the table. It was shaped like a carpenter's smoothing plane, approximately a foot long and four inches high; but it was clearly intended for domestic rather than craft use, since inscribed upon it was the phrase When with Long Grinding, Naturs Tools Are Spent: To Shave the Cheese, Art Found This Instrument. It is doubtful that such slicers were commercially manufactured, and this example may be unique.

## Voiders

The inventory of the Colonel Robert Oliver estate, made at Dorchester, Massachusetts, soon after his death in 1763, listed a "voider," which was a wooden box or tray used to collect waste at the conclusion of a meal. The contents of trenchers and platters would be scraped into the voider and thus removed from the festive board. Perhaps it was the first version of what we know as the "silent butler." A secondary use is reflected in Cumming's English dictionary of 1730, where voiders are described as being painted vessels intended to hold sweetmeats.

# Washing and ironing utensils

Early clothing presented problems for the housewife. The work clothes were heavy and often dirt-stained from the fields. Better garments were ruffled, highly starched, and often extremely fragile. It was some time before the first crude washing machines and commercial soaps appeared. In the interim, the work was done laboriously with soft soap and muscle.

### Leach barrels, tubs, and soap sticks

The making of soap was itself a major job. Once or twice a year oven and fireplace ashes were converted to lye, which was used as a base for soft soap. The leach barrel employed was made from a hollowed log section two or three feet long. Generally this barrel had no bottom and its lower edge was notched. Alternate layers of straw, lime, and ashes were placed in the receptacle above a grass and twig mat. Rainwater was poured through the mix, seeping out the bottom as lye. Leach barrels have not survived in any great number. They were not attractive or usable for any other purpose and were discarded when no longer needed.

Generally the barrel rested on a stone block with a groove cut into it. Draining lye passed down this into a lye tub, which was a staved and hooped vessel two feet in diameter and a foot high. Lye barrels were in common use until 1850. John Eaton of Jaffrey, New Hampshire, was making them in the 1770s, and the cooper Purdon Keith of West Bridgewater, Massachusetts, sold such items for $1.75 each in 1831.

When of proper strength, lye was mixed with household grease in a soap or "sope" tub such as the one owned by John Farrington at Dedham, Massachusetts, in 1676. A long wooden stick, usually of sweet-smelling sassafras, was employed in working the odoriferous contents until they reached the right consistency. The lye-induced bleaching of their wood readily distinguishes these stirrers from similar long blunt implements.

## Soft soap barrels and scoops

A squat soft soap barrel was used to store the year's supply. A "soap barrell" of this nature was among the possessions of Nathaniel Draper of Roxbury, Massachusetts, in 1767, and every homestead would have had one or more. Today they are seldom identified.

Crude boxlike handled scoops were used in removing soap from the barrels. These utensils were hand-carved and, as may be seen from figure 41, seldom more than a hollowed-out wooden block. They are readily distinguishable from the finely shaped scoops used in other areas of the house.

## Scrubbing sticks and washboards

Only in the earliest days did settlers resort to Indian methods by washing their clothes in a neighboring stream, where they were beaten with sticks upon a handy rock. Even then it was more likely that the scrubbing stick was employed. Typically, the scrubber was about two feet long and half a foot wide with a short handle. It was shaped much like a corrugated cricket paddle with deep ridges cut across one side of the body (see fig. 51). Clothing was soaped and rubbed back and forth across these indentations.

Whereas the scrubbing stick was European in origin, the colonists themselves appear to have devised the washboard. The earliest were wide slabs of corrugated wood with attached end boards terminating in feet. Later models had spool-turned columns riding on steel rods. Examples of both are seen in figure 51. They were easier to use than sticks and have been manufactured in quantity for many years. Armes and Dallam

FIGURE 51 Above left to right, *washboard with movable rollers, scrubbing stick, washboard;* below, *clothes or wash tongs.*

of San Francisco, California, made thousands of washboards between 1858 and 1892, and every area of the country had similar manufactories. L.H. Mace and Co. still listed all-wood washboards in 1883, at $1.20 per dozen. However, by that time most of these devices were metal-faced.

## Washtubs

Washtubs were made of staves locked together with nailed hoops. They had two short handles carved out of extended staves and an inset bottom. A well-made example is illustrated in figure 52. As early as 1771, Samuel Gardner of Brookline, Massachusetts, had such tubs in his home; and the cooper John Crawford of Davenport, New York, specialized in them during the 1850s. In 1856, the Niagara Pail and Tub Factory at Buffalo, New York offered wash tubs at $10.00 per dozen.

FIGURE 52  Left, *clothes pounder;* right, *staved washtub.*

## Dolly pins and clothes pounders

Garments were placed in a tub of hot soapy water and stirred to remove clinging dirt. The earliest device employed was the dolly pin, or clothes maul, a heavy wooden club with right-angle grooves set into the base and a crossbar handle. A housewife thrust the dolly into a tub of clothing and twisted it about in the manner of a primitive washing machine agitator. Warren Kimball of Jaffrey, New Hampshire, made clothes mauls for nearly forty years, from 1865 to 1902.

Clothes pounders were more sophisticated. They consisted of a long rod set into a circular or square base, which was formed to produce suction. In some cases this was achieved by hollowing out the block so that it was much like a modern plunger. Another technique involved drilling a series of holes into a square head. A patented version had a container for soap. As the pounder was worked up and down in a tub of clothing, soapsuds emerged through the drilled openings.

A semicircular agitator with vertical handle was also employed. This device, which is shown in figure 52, was rocked back and forth, in the wet wash to remove dirt particles.

## Washing machines

The exhausting labor involved in washing with a scrubboard or clothes pounder encouraged the introduction of mechanical alternatives. The first washing machine was patented in 1805, and by 1883 over 1,700 variations had obtained patent office approval.

Primitive models were of wood, consisting of a square box enclosing wooden paddles, which were turned by gearing them to an exterior handle. The water and strong soap had a deleterious effect on this material, and many a household regretted its introduction to "modern" methods. A correspondent to *Rural Magazine*, a nineteenth-century agricultural publication, declared that:

> The people have been so abominably cheated and gulled by the endless variety of these machines, it is difficult to attract their attention to any one, however excellent. Almost every bungler who can make a lumber box or an oxsled has invented them and most of them require the power of an ox to use them at all.

A wide variety of these early implements are found in local and regional museums. As the nineteenth century progressed, metal replaced wood in their construction, leading to development of the contemporary washer.

## Bleaching and dye tubs

The use of artificial whiteners was not unknown to our ancestors. Birch or other wood ash was boiled in hot water to produce a crude bleach. A large bleach tub was filled with clothing and the liquid was poured over them, draining out through several holes in the tub bottom. Two or three rinsings were generally sufficient. The few of these vessels found are themselves thoroughly bleached.

Lacking commercial dyes, housewives made their own from bark and wild plants. The ingredients were boiled in an iron kettle and poured into a dye tub, into which the materials to be stained were dipped. The usual dye tub was about eighteen inches high, staved and hooped with a shape tapering out to the base. They were traditionally kept near the hearth and often served as an extra seat, since they were covered.

In order to avoid the effect of bleach or dye on the skin, clothing so treated was often handled with a large pair of wooden pinchers that resembled in appearance and action a giant pair of pliers. These are rarely found now and generally bear the effects of dye or bleach. A representative pair from the collection of the Farmers' Museum at Cooperstown, New York, is shown in figure 51.

## Clothespins and clothesline winders

While the first drying laundry might have been draped on tree limbs or bushes, it was not long before clothespins became available to the colonists. The earlier were hand carved of birch or pine; later examples were turned on a lathe. The whittled examples were blunt and unfinished. Mid-nineteenth-century pins were often well turned, and manufacturers such as Ephraim Murdock, of Winchendan, Massachusetts (active in the 1840s), took pride in offering an attractive as well as durable product.

The jute line used to hang clothes was stored on a frame consisting either of a ladder-shaped framework with center-turning handle (see fig. 53) or two such ladders joined at right angles, forming a Maltese cross. Similar frames (fig. 42), are still used by fishermen for storing and drying line, so it is seldom possible to determine the exact age of these.

FIGURE 53  Left to right, *rope bed wrench, (two) foot warmers, clothesline winder.*

## Clothes-drying racks

In the days before automatic dryers a variety of wooden frames were used for undercover drying during inclement weather. The Pensacola Historical Society collection includes a simple drying rack of pine made in Texas in the middle of the last century. It is formed of two flat pine boards joined at top and bottom by pairs of wooden rods. Wet clothing was draped over each rod.

In 1883, L.H. Mace and Co. offered Booth's Patent Clothes Dryer, a set of four to six upright frames radiating off a central shaft about which they could be folded for storage purposes. They were described as "made very light, yet substantial, with circular bolts running through the bars, with thumb nuts to regulate them, so that they may be made to stand at any angle, well braced." The four-arm dryer sold at $9 a dozen, the six-arm one at $12 a dozen.

Clothes horses from three to seven feet high were also used in drying. They were manufactured in three ladderlike sections hinged together so that they could be folded one upon the other. These devices were made in some quantity and appear often in modern collections.

## Towel arms and extension racks

Towels were dryed on towel arms—sets of three rods attached to a metal base that might be screwed into a wall. An iron pin running vertically through the rods enabled them to be swiveled back and forth. Mace offered two varieties of such arms, both made of black walnut. The plainest sold for $1.50 a dozen, and better grades listed at $2.00 and at $3.25, the latter for a set with a malleable iron base and silver rod tips.

Walnut extension racks with seven to thirteen knobs to hang clothing on were also a Mace product. They opened and closed like an accordian and were nailed to an entry or porch wall to accommodate spare garments.

## Smoothing boards and sticks

Before introduction of the flat iron, linens were pressed and dryed through use of smoothing sticks and boards. A sheet or spread was wrapped tight about a round rod two or three inches in diameter and three feet long. A smoothing board, which was a flat stick several feet in length, slightly curved and sometimes with round indentations, was then employed to smooth the material. The technique was still known in the late nineteenth century and the housewife's procedure was then described as follows:

> At ironing time, after sprinkling each garment, she would roll up the garment and then she would place the rolled-up garment on the kitchen table. Grabbing both ends of this wooden ironing aid she would place it on the garment and roll back and forth at a slight angle. This action not only distributed the moisture evenly but also softened the material, eliminating many wrinkles. . . .

The smoothing stick upon which the material was rolled is easily confused with a stirrer or early rolling pin.

The smoothing board (fig. 54) may also be confused with

FIGURE 54 Above left, *knife box;* right, *smoothing board;* below, *pumice box.*

another household utensil, the scrubbing stick. Each may be corrugated. However, the former is nearly always curved rather than flat, has rounded rather than sharp ridging, and frequently bears a carved, flat-iron style handle.

## Bosom, skirt, and sleeve boards

The firm of North and Bogue at Cohoes, New York, advertised "drying boards" during the 1860s and 1870s. There were at least three types of such boards, all used to facilitate pressing of the many flounces and frills prevalent in Victorian style.

In 1883, L.H. Mace and Co. offered coffin-shaped bosom boards at $1.70 per dozen. Skirt boards, looking like handleless paddles and ranging in length from three to six feet, were also available, as were pine or black walnut sleeve boards. The latter were two feet long and no more than four inches wide. When properly drilled they made excellent cribbage boards, a function served by many of the remaining examples. Bosom forms became chopping or pastry boards, and few of these remain despite the vast number manufactured.

# Flax-spinning implements

It is difficult for us to conceive, in these days of haberdashery chains and factory outlets, the vast amount of labor that went into the manufacture of colonial clothing. The rural family not only made its own garments, but also planted, raised, and prepared the raw material from which these were produced.

In the northeast most people wore linen, made from the flax plant. Flax seeds were sowed in the spring, producing a tall wiry plant with blue flowers. At maturity, in July or August, these plants were pulled up and allowed to dry for a few days.

## Ripple combs and flax brakes

The bundles of dried stalks were next drawn through a ripple comb, a plank into which two rows of iron or whittled wooden teeth were set. By this process the seed bolls were torn off to be saved for another crop. Ripple combs are relatively uncommon today, though many must have once existed.

Having been rippled, the stalks were tied in bundles and soaked in water to rot the leaves, which were then removed. The naked stalks were once more bundled, dried, and then "broken" on a flax brake. This was a massive wooden beam or log with its top cut down to leave a raised section at each end and parallel wooden slats along the center. An upper jaw with matching, meshing slots could be shut down upon the base like a jackknife blade. The entire structure stood on four legs. Bunches of flax were laid on the lower section and crushed by the operator's pressing down the top. This tiring exercise softened and separated the flax fibers and facilitated removal of the woody core. A flax brake was in the inventory of Nathaniel

Draper, who died at Roxbury, Massachusetts, in 1767; and flax brakes were among the more common items found in pre-1800 homes.

## Swingling knives and blocks

The broken core and bark fibers were separated from the long strands of flax by scraping with a swingling or scutching knife. This was a carved wooden implement resembling a sword. The example, illustrated in figure 55, which is in the collection of the Farmers' Museum at Cooperstown, New York, has a well-worked blade some two feet long and a curved handle of great delicacy.

The fibers were laid over the swingling block, which was simply a flat board set into a rough wooden base, and the

FIGURE 55 Above left, *Niddy Noddy;* above right, *loom shuttle with bobbin;* center, *swingling knife;* below left, *set of wool cards;* below right, *loom spool.*

knife was scraped along them to remove adhering particles. It was a dusty and tedious job but absolutely essential.

## Hatchels

Once cleaned, the now-flexible fibers were again bundled and laid in a wooden trough to be beaten with a beetle, a massive wooden pestle whose abrasive action served to further soften the vegetable issue. Such a utensil was among the possessions of Theophilus Eaton at New Haven, Connecticut, in 1657.

The fibrous material was next drawn through a series of fine iron teeth set into a wooden block. This device, called a hatchel, or hetchel, may be distinguished from the ripple comb in that it is much thicker, with as many as two or three dozen closely set spikes; in some cases there were two separate clusters of these, one more tightly bunched than the other for finer work. An early form appears in figure 56.

The purpose of hatcheling was to divide the fibers into long silken filaments that could be spun into thread. As the flax was worked through the spikes, shorter strands fell out. These were called tow and were used in spinning a coarse thread for bagging and rough cloth. The longer, better-quality lengths were hatcheled several times to produce a fine, uniform thread.

The hatchel is a very old instrument. There was one among the possessions of New Haven's Theophilus Eaton, and the form persisted until the end of the cottage flax industry. Most of these tools were made of maple, birch, or oak. In better examples the teeth were first driven through a small board and this then was attached to the main base. Less skillfully done are ones where the nails are simply driven straight through the baseboard. These latter often split during use.

The hatchel base may be shaped like a breadboard with a hole in each end by which it was attached to a bench or table. It may also be oval or round. Decorated examples are not unknown, and dated specimens appear. There are several that bear the mark Aaron Manning, 1824.

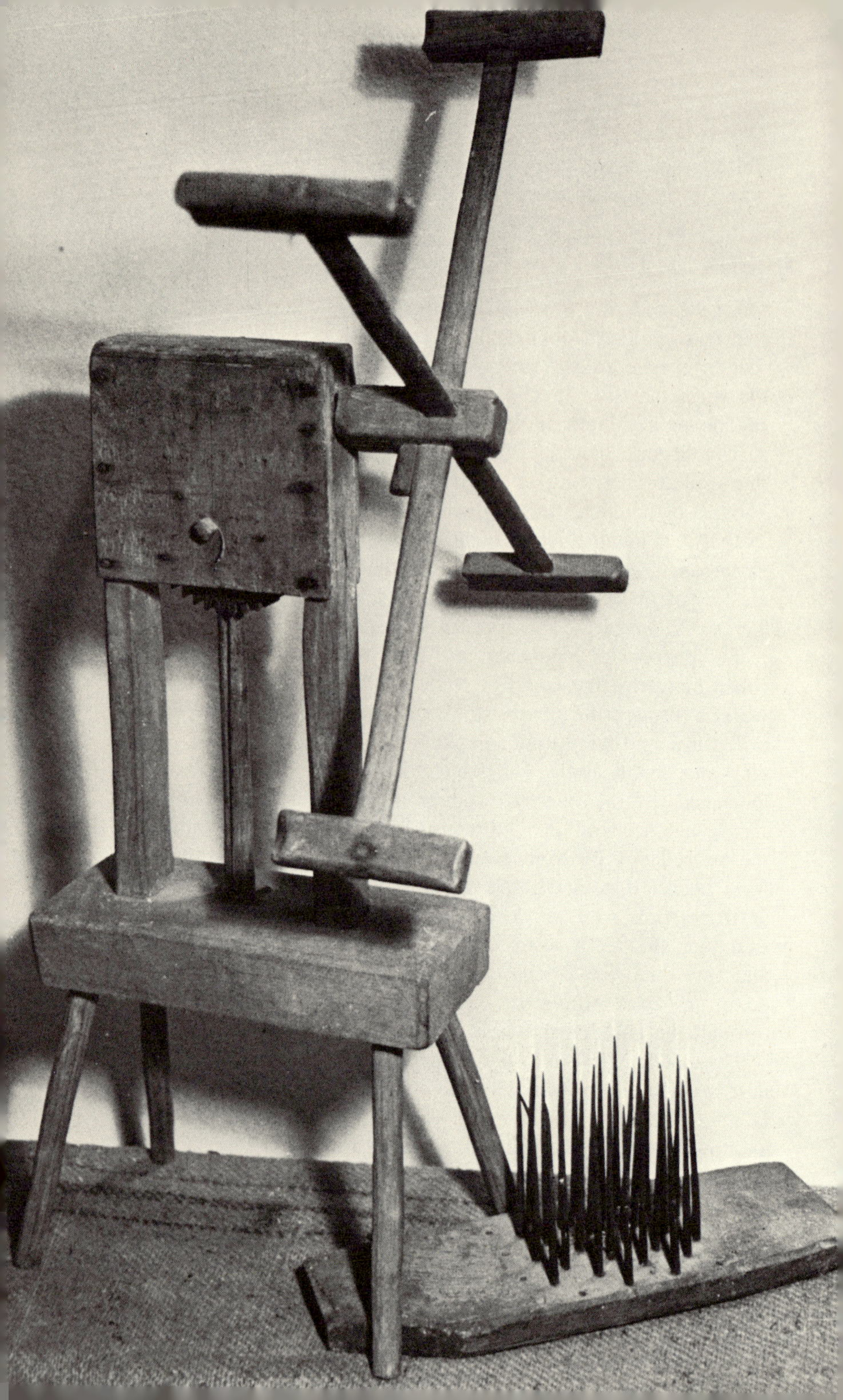

## Flax wheels and clock reels

The coarse flax fibers were spun into thread on a flax wheel. The raw material was wound on a small treen spindle, from which, by the turning of the wheel, it was twisted into a long, even thread that was stored on bobbins.

*Figure 57.*

FIGURE 56 (facing page)   Left, *clock reel;* right, *hatchel.*

Flax wheels (fig. 57) are similar in appearance and function to the larger wool spinning wheels. They sit on four splayed legs that are often well turned. The wheel may be painted or scratch-decorated, and dates and names are frequently encountered, since many of these pieces were made as gifts for wives and sweethearts. The earliest flax wheels were imported from Europe, but they were widely made here from the seventeenth century on. One of the earliest manufacturers known is John Eaton, who was active at Jaffrey, New Hampshire, during the 1770s.

Bobbin-wound thread was counted off in measured amounts, hired spinners being paid by the quantity they could produce. A tally was kept by use of the clock reel, which consisted of an X shaped frame attached to a vertical block into which was built a crude counting device. This all sat on a simple table base with four attached, turned legs. The reel shown in figure 56 is representative.

Thread was stripped from a bobbin and wound about the turning X frame of the reel; each revolution caused a metal "clicker" to sound. When the worker had heard forty such clicks, she knew that a "knot," the smallest unit of measure, had been wound off. Forty knots equaled a skein, and only the best spinners could produce more than two of these in a day. The record holder, perhaps, was Eleanor Fry of East Greenwich, Rhode Island, who is said to have spun seven skeins in a single day in 1777.

## Bucking tubs

The raw linen thread had a tan color not considered desirable in clothing, so it was bleached. Several days' soaking in warm water was followed by a thorough rinsing. Then the skeins were bleached several times with a solution of hot water and wood ashes or slaked lime. For this operation a squat, wide staved tub known as a bucking tub was used. It was usually about two feet high and at least three in diameter, and was bound with iron or wooden hoops. Remaining specimens show a distinctly pale interior owing to the action of bleaching compounds.

# Wool spinning and weaving

There were over 3,000 sheep in Massachusetts by 1645, and raising of the animals for their wool was encouraged by custom and law. In New England a sheep killed by a dog had to be paid for twice over, while the Virginia colony paid a reward in tobacco to anyone producing a single yard of woolen cloth.

Fleece, the bunching hair sheared from sheep, was first carefully picked over to remove tar, burdocks, and other foreign bodies. It was then sorted and placed in net bags to be dyed, usually a shade of blue, yellow, or red.

### Wool cards and combs

The wool was then greased with hog fat or oil from the rape plant so that it might slide easily through the teeth of a set of wool cards. These were thin, rectangular board slabs with an attached handle. To the face of each was attached an oblong piece of hard leather set with many fine wire teeth in the manner of a hairbrush. A pair of such cards appears in figure 55. A skilled carder could take tufts of wool and work them between the cards until they were stretched to their full length. Next they were rolled into small balls suitable for spinning.

Wool cards were at first handmade. Such were the "Two Paire Cardes" listed among the possessions of Dedham's John Farrington in 1676. However, by the late eighteenth century these implements were made in small factories.

For finer work, large wool combs in the shape of the letter "T" with several dozen teeth a foot or more long were used. A longer thread or staple was achieved with these devices, but the work was most tedious and demanding.

## Wool spinning wheels and wheel drivers

In 1688, John Richards of Dedham, Massachusetts, owned "1 Woolen wheele." It is likely that most of his neighbors had similar devices to spin locks of carded wool into thread, since the big wheels were made throughout the country. At Zoar, Ohio, the emigrant German turner Conrad Dienman made spinning wheels marked with his name from 1820 to 1860. In Texas, Joseph Jackson & Sons, of Lexington, produced a serviceable type from Civil War days until the end of the last century.

Wool spinning was quite similar in technique to flax work. The end of a carded wool roll was wound onto the wheel spindle. The wheel was then revolved by use of a wheel driver (also known as "speed boy," or "finger"), which was a lathe-turned wooden rod about nine inches long with a slight groove an inch or two from the head to catch and so propel the wheel. As the wheel spun, it twisted the long yarn onto the spindle. As in flax spinning, count was kept of the thread produced by means of a clock reel.

Spinning wheels are today in great demand as decorative pieces, and large numbers are being imported from central Europe, where they were used until recently. American examples may often be identified through names, of manufacturers or owners, scratched or stamped into the wood. Like the smaller flax wheel, these articles are frequently embellished with gouge carving or painted motifs on the wheel, legs, and frame.

## The niddy noddy

Prior to 1750 much wool was spun by use of a hand reel, or niddy noddy, (fig. 55) which consisted of three pieces of wood: a central shaft and two T-shaped crossarms, one at each end, lying at right angles to each other. The odd shape gave rise to the old riddle:

> Niddy noddy, niddy noddy
> Two heads and one body.

The tool was used in the following manner. Gripping the central shaft, the spinner wound yarn in a rotating motion from end to end upon the reel. The prescribed length of the device corresponded to a unit of the knot as previously defined. Thus, a certain number of turns would equal a knot, and twenty knots a skein. The end result was the same, but the same amount of thread required far more effort to achieve.

This problem must have weighed upon some women, for the early Boston chronicles record the case of a spinner who was fined and imprisoned for shortening the shank of her niddy noddy, thus lessening the length of her windings and the capacity of her skeins.

The niddy noddy is an attractive form with an interesting history. It is, accordingly, often found in antiques shops. Most examples are of some age, and many are set together with wooden pegs. Dates and initials and modest scratch carving increase the interest in some of these pieces.

## Swifts

Homespun yarn, both linen and woolen, was woven into a wide variety of materials. The skeins of prepared thread were wound onto a revolving cylindrical framework of thin wooden slats called a swift. These were adjustable to accommodate varying quantities of yarn. Some swifts were attached by a central shaft to a heavy block base, but most terminated in a turned treen clamp by which they might be fastened to a tabletop. A fine and possibly Shaker-made example is shown in figure 58.

The Shakers were famous for their wooden swifts; and in 1883 L.H. Mace and Co. offered these in three sizes: small,

*Figure 58.*

medium, and large. The prices per dozen were, respectively, $10.50, $11.25 and $12.00. Because of their fragility, a limited number of such devices have survived to the present day. These, because of their attractive form and frequent decoration (including bone or shell inlay and carving), are in great demand.

Figure 59.

## Spools, bobbins, and quilling wheels

From the swift, thread was transferred to spools and bobbins used on the hand loom. Spools (fig. 55) were, as the name implies, turned wooden thread holders with flaring flat ends. They were about five inches long and held the yarn used to form the warp (the thread that ran the long way) of a woven fabric. On occasion, they bore the name or initials of the manufacturer, adding interest to an otherwise prosaic item.

Bobbins or quills were narrow, hollow wooden tubes upon which was wrapped the woof, or weft, threads, those which were woven back and forth across the warp threads. Among the many nineteenth-century manufacturers of these simple items was the small firm of North and Boque in Cohoes, New York.

A small machine of simple construction called a quilling wheel (fig. 59) was used to convey yarn from the swift to bobbins and spools. These were set in a specially prepared frame at one side of the wheel and then filled from the swift by turning a crank at the side of the quilling wheel.

## Skarnes and shuttles

A large number of spools and quills were required to weave a single piece of fabric. As the former were filled with thread, they were stored on a skarne, or scarne, which was a narrow rectangular rack with removable iron rods running through the horizontal pieces. Each weaving spool had a hole through its shaft so that the iron rods might be removed from the skarne, slipped through the shafts, and then replaced, holding the spools securely until needed. An unusual skarne in a private collection has vertical end posts made from the well-turned legs of an eighteenth-century gateleg table.

Bobbins were stored in a bobbin basket (see Basketry section), then placed for use in boat-shaped containers called shuttles. These were made of apple or box tree wood and, like spools, often marked by their makers. The bobbin snapped into place on a metal attachment within the shuttle and turned so that thread might be drawn off as needed. After 1825 most shuttles were produced in factories. L.S. Watson and Co. of Leicester, Massachusetts, one of the largest manufacturers, turned out vast numbers of these receptacles between 1842 and 1952. That the business continued so far into the twentieth century reflects the fact that in many areas of the world hand-weaving is still a viable industry. A standard factory produced shuttle is shown in figure 55.

## Tape looms

The weaving loom was a massive piece of furniture with vertical sections often seven feet high. It frequently occupied an entire room and, hence, has little place in a book on smaller woodenware. There were, however, miniature devices known as tape or braid looms, or, quaintly, as "gallus-frames," alluding to their use in suspender weaving.

Such looms were no more than shaped boards with narrow slots cut into them and, across the center of these, a horizontal series of small holes burned through with a hot rod. The warp

FIGURE 60   Left, *tape loom;* right, *boxed braid loom.*

threads were passed through these tiny apertures and the weft threads were woven across them with the loom held in a vertical position. A somewhat more sophisticated version was the braid loom, which was permanently fixed in a boxlike container with revolving wheels on which the thread was stored. In either case, the product was a narrow band of woven fabric. Both tape and braid looms appear in figure 60.

Tape looms were once used as "spare time" activity by most women and girls, so many examples have come down to us. They are often dated or decorated. One in the collection of the Farmers' Museum at Cooperstown, New York, bears the date 1669. Another, in a private collection is incised with the motherly admonition "Mind Yor Work."

# Sewing and embroidery treen

With the exception of needles, nearly everything used by the colonial seamstress was made of wood. It was an ideal material for the craft, being both light and easily formed. While treen sewing birds have been eagerly sought for years, most other sewing implements in the medium attract little collector attention.

### Sewing birds

Finely turned sewing birds or clamps are among the most attractive of treen ware. They are composed of two sections, a C clamp similar to those used by carpenters and a small dishtop pedestal. The bird was fastened to a tabletop with the screw clamp turned flush up against it, while fabric to be sewn was pinned to a small cushion secured to the pedestal top. Craftsmen made many of these sewing devices and often lavished a great deal of decorative attention on them. A rare burl specimen in the collection of Devere Card of Hamilton, New York, terminates in a finial similar to those found on eighteenth-century ladder-back chairs.

Later clamps were made from cast iron in the shape of a bird with material gripped by spring tension in the beak—hence the term *sewing bird*.

### Thimbles and thimble holders

Lathe-turned wooden thimbles were a poor woman's substitute for the silver or gold finger-protectors worn by wealthier members of the community. They were frequently decorated with incised initials, dates, and decorative devices. Circles, stars, crosshatching, and floral patterns are most common. American examples are at times hard to distinguish from similar thimbles made in Europe.

Lovely footed urns a few inches high were used to store thimbles or pills. They had close-fitting tops with acorn finials and were turned with great care. Ring, scroll, and groove cutting were employed to create attractive patterns on the plain or shellacked receptacles.

Hiram Pease of Lake County, Ohio, manufactured walnut and maple thimble holders during the second half of the nineteenth century. Several examples of his work are in midwestern collections.

## Spool holders

Sewing thread was stored in a spool holder, another interesting late-nineteenth-century form. Such containers were turned on a lathe from two separate pieces of wood, one of which fit into the other. The top and bottom portions were cut back to a narrow center shaft, the upper portion of which was hollow to provide a thimble storage spot. Wires were placed in the cutout gallery about the column and the spools of thread were stacked on these wires. The upper portion of the holder terminated in a pincushion; and in larger specimens there was often a button drawer or compartment at the base.

Hiram Pease also manufactured spool holders and charged only six cents apiece for them in the late 1800s. His products are characterized by bold turnings and an attractive finish.

## Needle boxes

Another midwestern specialty was the Victorian needle box, a barrel-shaped receptacle two or three inches tall with an inset lid. They, too, were lathe-turned with raised rings as decoration and a shallow, molded foot. The lids were completely plain, waferlike pieces of wood. Although, sometimes they were found painted, most needle boxes were varnished or waxed.

## Buttons

Wood was certainly the first material used to make buttons, and its use persists to the present. The earliest American examples were carefully whittled out of maple or fruitwood, with the threading holes burned through by a hot rod. Later, factory-made buttons were stamped out with a heavy press. While only a few earlier buttons were decorated (usually through scratch technique), later examples often bore machine-impressed motifs. Few colonial button makers are known, but it appears that Samuel and Jonathan Osborn of Weare Center, New Hampshire, worked in the trade during the last decade of the eighteenth century.

## Darning knobs

Egg-shaped darning knobs with short, turned handles are seen today both as antiques and as modern implements. A piece of torn or worn material was slipped over the knob head to facilitate darning or stitching. Earlier examples tend to be larger than their modern counterparts and were sometimes painted red or blue. Hiram Pease of Lake County, Ohio, made plain varnished knobs, while Pennsylvania's Joseph Lehn carefully decorated his with scratch carving and polychrome design.

## Lap boards

Lap boards appear frequently in antiques shops but are seldom recognized. They are usually about three feet wide by two to three high with a shallow half-moon cut out of one long side. They were intended to rest on a woman's lap, providing a flat surface on which to do cutting, basting, or writing.

Their popularity in the late nineteenth century is attested to by Mace's 1883 catalog, which lists three separate models; an "American Fancy" made from several different types of wood with facsimile inlay, a plain white pine board, and a folding version constructed from alternating strips of black walnut and pine fastened to a back cloth. The latter sold for $9 a dozen and were noted to be "finished nicely and have stamped upon them a yard measure; convenient, strong and will not warp."

## Embroidery yarn holders

Skeins of embroidery yarn were hung on a two-piece rack for storage. The upper and lower sections of this rack were joined by numerous pairs of cords, and the skeins of yarn were laid between these where they could be kept straight and ready for use. The holder itself was hung from the ceiling on an iron hook.

The interesting thing about this device is that the flat wooden sections were often intricately carved with moldings, stylized sunflowers, and other floral figures. In volume I of his *Furniture of the Pilgrim Century*, Wallace Nutting illustrates a pair of hickory yarn holders made in Connecticut at the end of the seventeenth century. Examples outside museum collections are very rare.

# Decorated boxes

Among the most collectible of all treen are decorated boxes. At one time or another probably every box type has been embellished through incising, painting, or application of designed paper and inlaid materials. However, it is evident that decorators favored certain types. Bandboxes and bride's boxes are generally so adorned, while decoration is rare in common storage boxes.

## Bandboxes

In the seventeenth century, wood veneer or cardboard boxes were used to store men's linen neckbands. These round or oval receptacles, some as large as suitcases, were covered with wood-block-printed paper, either contemporary wall covering or a specially designed covering. The first examples were relatively conservative; but when women began to use them for cap and bonnet storage, these containers assumed a more lively appearance.

Typically, bandbox paper was printed in gray or white on a soft green, yellow, or blue background. A wide variety of scenes and designs appeared on the containers. Horses, stagecoaches, trains, canal boats, sailing ships, and even balloons were featured, as well as historic sites and events. Among the most interesting locations pictured are the capital at Washington, New York's City Hall and Convent Gardens, and the main university buildings at Harvard and Yale.

Patriotic motifs such as the eagle and cannon were common, as were re-creations of memorable events such as the surrender of Cornwallis, the battle of New Orleans, and Washington's inaugural address.

Throughout the middle of the last century, bandbox manufacture was big business with hundreds of separate shops employed. In New York City, Thomas Day, Jr., and Barnard Andrews were active in the 1850s, while Philadelphia's Henry Barnes was a contemporary. But, perhaps, the best-known maker was Hannah Davis of Jaffrey, New Hampshire.

The daughter of a well known New Hampshire turner, Hannah Davis worked diligently to establish herself in box manufacture. She went into the woods, selected suitable spruce trees, cut them down, and had them dragged home. There she sliced the logs into veneer of a suitable width, bent the strips in a mold, and nailed them in place while still green. Tops and bottoms of seasoned pine were added, and the exterior was covered with decorative wallpaper. Newspapers of the period served as a lining; and today boxes are often accurately dated through examination of these old papers. A label, Warranted Nailed Bandboxes Manufactured by Hannah Davis East Jaffrey, N.H., was placed on the cover of each container.

After the boxes were finished, Ms. Davis piled them on a wagon and drove down into Lowell or Manchester, the valley industrial towns, where she sold them to mill girls. The usual price was twelve cents to fifty cents each, depending upon size. Today, choice examples may sell for one thousand times these figures.

## Brides' boxes

A quaint and lovely oval box was used to house the bride's wedding bonnet. Instead of being nailed or pegged into shape as with most such containers, brides' boxes (fig. 61) were steamed, bent, and then sewn together with fine reed or splint. Their exteriors, including the overlapping lid, were painted in a pastel ground upon which floral motifs, such as garlands of roses or lilies, were imposed. The receptacles ranged in length from twelve to eighteen inches and were three to six inches high. Pious sayings were often painted on the top or sides.

FIGURE 61  Upper left, *grain measure;* upper right, *bride's box;* lower left, *Shaker herb box;* lower right, *pill boxes.*

Documented American brides' boxes are for the most part from Pennsylvania. They were also widely made in Western Europe, particularly in Switzerland and Germany. Since a good number of these boxes have been imported, it is often difficult to distinguish a domestic example.

### Pantry boxes

During the nineteenth century, miniature dometop boxes were made in imitation of the Victorian trunk. While termed "pantry boxes" by some, they were, in fact, used for various purposes in different parts of the house. A splendid example, sold at New York's Sotheby Parke-Bernet gallery in November 1972, was initialed and dated 1823. Drapery and swags in ochre and red were figured on a dark green ground, and the interior contained two tills and a small drawer. Another, adorned with polychrome flowers on a marbelized background, was made in 1827 for Abigail Fisk of Springfield, Massachusetts, and was signed by the decorator, J. Sawin/Coach Painter/Wmsett. These pieces were frequently lined with wallpaper in the manner of bandboxes. The close-up in figure 62 shows the detailed decoration with which pantry boxes were adorned.

FIGURE 62  *Detail, painted bureau box.*

## Bureau boxes

Bureau or trinket boxes, like pantry boxes, are small, rarely more than eighteen inches long, have a hinged lid, and are ornately decorated. They are distinguished by a flat top and rectangular shape, but a few oval examples are known. Painted figures and scenes may be confined to the cover with the rest of the container done in sponged blue or red. There is a remarkable example at historic Old Deerfield, Massachusetts; its lid is covered with a detailed painting of Indians attacking a settlement. It appears to be illustrative of the 1780 Tory and Indian raid, which left most of Deerfield in ruins.

### Gum boxes

A form confined to the lumbering woods of Maine and northern New Hampshire is the gum box or "book." These boxes average five inches by four inches and are made from poplar or ash carved to look like a miniature book. After initial shaping, the interior of the wood block is hollowed out and grooves cut in the top and bottom. Thin slices of cedar slipped into these channels provide sliding endpieces.

The exterior of the book is scratch-carved in religious or sentimental motifs such as flowers, hearts, sunbursts, and women's names. A coat of varnish or stain completes the job, and the container is then filled with spruce gum and given as a gift to a wife or sweetheart.

Most gum boxes date from the twentieth century, the making of such objects having been a popular bunkhouse pastime in the lumbering camps up until the Second World War.

### Cookie boxes

In Pennsylvania, turned circular cookie boxes were popular. These were nearly a foot in diameter with round wooden lids that fit into a hole a few inches wide cut in the top of the box. The lids had a carved lift handle, and the sides of the container were frequently painted or incised with floral or animal forms. Birds were common, particularly doves and peacocks.

### Candle boxes

From the earliest period, tallow candles were stored in rectangular pine boxes with sliding lids. These containers were made to accommodate one or several dozen candles and were dovetailed or put together with wooden pegs. Frequent references to such boxes appear in early inventories, and records indicate that the cabinetmaker Nathaniel Dominy IV made one for Joseph Robbins of East Hampton, Long Island, in 1790.

FIGURE 63  *Decorated candle box.*

Most decorated candle boxes are painted rather than scratch-carved. The Metropolitan Museum in New York City has an interesting specimen almost entirely covered with rich purple grapes and green leaves. Most examples, however, were less ornate. In figure 63 a simple late nineteenth-century box bears the name of its maker, A. E. Burdick. The writing appears in black upon a tan ground with red arrow devices at the corners.

## Pencil boxes

Lead or slate pencils were stored in another receptacle with sliding top. Pencil boxes were narrower and lower than candle boxes but basically similar in shape. They were manufactured from pine or walnut and often had two or more compartments separated by thin dividing panels. Decoration was usually paint or stencil, the latter technique being employed in factory-made examples of the late nineteenth century. Inlay, particularly mother-of-pearl, was also used. In Pennsylvania, geometric designs were gouged out of the surface and the spaces filled with clam shell or contrasting colored wood.

## Lather boxes

The wooden containers used with old-fashioned straightedge razors were called lather or shaving boxes. They were frequently adorned with lithographs or watercolors of Victorian beauties, such as Jenny Lind. The lithograph was glued to the wood surface then covered with protective shellac. Malby, Fowler and Son of Northfield, Connecticut, manufactured similar boxes in the 1830s and 1840s.

## Cottonwood boxes

In New Mexico, soft cottonwood was dovetailed together in the form of square or rectangular storage boxes. It was then blackened with a mixture of tar and pitch and inlaid with designs in wheat straw, which adhered to the sticky coating.

## Ballot boxes and cashboxes

Two other containers with sliding tops were ballot boxes and cashboxes. The former was a square or slightly oblong dovetailed receptacle with a slot in the domed lid through which a paper ballot might be passed. Although they were never made in any great number, at least one artisan, Abner Taylor of Lee, Massachusetts (ca. 1806–24), is known to have advertised such a form.

Extremely long double-compartment boxes with two sliding lids were used as cashboxes or change boxes. The gouge-cut

FIGURE 64   Left, *cash box;* right, *ballot box.*

finger holes cut into the covers to facilitate their removal differed in number on the two sides, probably to help identify which was the coin and which the paper money chamber.

While normally painted in solid color or simply vanished, both ballot boxes and cashboxes may be found decorated. Incised geometrics are most common, and a few Pennsylvania and Ohio polychrome pieces are known. An undecorated example of each form is shown in figure 64.

# Utility boxes

Though many have vanished over the years, plain, undecorated boxes were at a time one of the most common forms in treen. Single receptacles and nests of boxes, each one slightly larger than the last, were used to store ground meal, spices, and baking soda, as well as buttons and other small household necessities.

Each individual size and form was standardized by manufacture on a carved wooden mold. Thinly shaved basswood, birch, or another flexible wood was used for the sides or "windings" of the container; and pine was universally approved for tops and bottoms. The veneer strip windings were soaked until flexible, then carefully wrapped about the mold and cut to size. The joint might be a series of finger-shaped laps, as in the so-called "Shaker boxes," or simply a vertical seam. In either case the chamfered wooden ends were nailed together with iron, copper, or lead nails. The area of the mold over which this nailing was done had previously been covered by a copper strip to protect the block.

The box top and bottom were at first cut out by hand after the form was marked with a compass on the pine stock. Later, in the small box mills, a heavy press was used to stamp out the appropriate sizes. In the earliest boxes, tiny square pegs were employed to join tops and bottoms to the windings. Later, round pegs and, finally, small nails came to serve the same purpose.

While one tends to think of this craft as being the domain of skilled individual craftsmen, each laboriously creating one box after another, it was in most cases an early form of mass-production. A description of the pillbox factory owned by Nathan Crary at Knox, New York, and active for a full century after 1806, indicates rather advanced techniques. The sides or windings were shaved from a wooden block by use of a horse-drawn flywheel with an attached plane against which the material was held. Windings were also precut to standard sizes, while tops and bottoms were stamped out by press in large quantities. Women and girls from neighboring farms, rather than turners or coopers, were employed at three to seven cents per hundred to put the boxes together. It is said that one of these operatives could assemble 1,600 to 1,800 containers in a day.

**Butter and cheese boxes**

Early boxes range in diameter from two inches up to twenty-four. The largest were used for storage of butter and cheese (the latter receptacles are discussed in detail in the section on Cheese Making). Many of these boxes bear evidence of handwork: quarter-inch-thick veneer windings, nails of irregular size, and unusual lap joinings. While some outsized oval containers are known, most large boxes were round. L.H. Mace and Co. was offering these throughout the 1880s in nests of five, varnished or plain. The former sold at $4.50 a dozen, the latter for a dollar less. While solid winding construction was most common, some butter containers were stave-made to allow for expansion and contraction of the moisture-laden contents.

**Herb, meal, and sugar boxes**

An intermediate sized box, ranging from twelve to eighteen inches across, served to contain herbs, meal, and sugar. The tight-fitting, overlapping lids common to these examples were most important to preserve the qualities of the herbs and to prevent rodents from damaging the meal.

Herb receptacles (an example appears in fig. 37) were usually oval rather than circular as were meal and sugar containers. Medicinal plants gathered from the fields, broken into short sections, and dried in rafter-hung bunches were then packed into herb boxes and stored until needed.

Sugar and meal boxes held relatively small quantities of commodities that were customarily packed in large tubs or barrels. Sugar crystals and grains of corn, rye, or oatmeal serve to identify the use of these receptacles. A "lot" of such boxes was in the estate of Boston's John Cogswell, who died in 1818.

## Spice boxes

When Grace Lloyd died at Chester, Pennsylvania, in 1760, she too had boxes among her possessions, in this case several dozen spice containers. Many other people must have maintained comparable supplies for these receptacles are, outside of cheese boxes, the most common of utility vessels. The fragrant odor of their former contents leaves no doubt as to their use.

While some are round, the majority of spice boxes are oval and vary in size from four inches up to a foot in diameter. They were primarily of maple, birch, or ash, though L.H. Mace and Co. sold black walnut ones for $8.50 a dozen in 1883. The spice box pictured in figure 37 is of probable Shaker origin, as is the herb box in figure 61.

It is among these containers that one most clearly sees the distinction between the so-called "Shaker Boxes" and others. It is clear that Shaker craftsmen at settlements in the eastern United States made a more or less standard oval box with from two to four "fingers" at the joint. These pointed termini were inserted into holes cut in the opposite side of the winding and then nailed into place (see fig. 65). A universal high quality is prevalant in these examples, something often lacking in other, particularly factory-made, boxes. The New Lebanon, New York, Shakers are known to have manufactured for sale to "the world" (as nonbelievers were designated) graduated

*Figure 65.*

sets of fingered boxes in groups of five, seven, nine, and twelve. Many of these were constructed by the coopers Ebenezer Cooley (active 1806–16) and John Farrington (active ca. 1800).

One cannot assume, however, that all such receptacles are Shaker-made. There were many other craftsmen fully capable of creating this form, and worldly examples identical to Shaker specimens have been identified. Thomas Annett of Rindge, New Hampshire, specialized in veneer spice boxes during the nineteenth century, as did J.C. Brown of Painesville, Ohio. There is no doubt, however, that the Shakers manifested a preference for the oval fingered shape, while most other coopers made the less complex round, vertical jointed box.

## Pillboxes

Tiniest of all these containers is the pillbox (see fig. 61). Some are only two inches across; and, even the largest are less than half a foot at the widest point. They are both round and oval. Because of the small sizes involved, these vessels were often

*Figure 66.*

joined with glue, or perhaps tiny copper nails, (fig. 66). They held a wide variety of medicines. The Crary shop at Knox, New York, produced receptacles stamped "Sherman's Cathartic Lozengers, New York" and "Dr. Ingoldsby's Vegetable Extract." Numerous other manufacturers employed box manufacturies to create boxes for their nostrums.

# Miscellaneous household treen

Many household utensils once manufactured of wood are now made of metal, glass, or pottery. Other items have fallen into disuse and have no contemporary parallel. Yet, a hundred years ago everything from powder horns to bedpans was carved or turned in treen.

## Soap dishes, washbowls, and towel rollers

A Victorian bedroom feature was the washstand or table. Often, the soap dish and washbowl placed thereon were of wood. The soap holder was usually a rectangular pine block with the interior gouged out. A coat of red or blue paint might cover the exterior. The interior would bear evidence of the corrosive lye used as a base for soft soap.

The washbowl was a relatively shallow turned vessel some sixteen inches in diameter, though any wooden bowl might, and often did, serve the purpose. Mark Marle of Jaffrey, New Hampshire, was manufacturing these items in the 1820s.

A towel roller was affixed to the wall adjacent to the washstand. The Philadelphia cabinetmaker David Evans advertised these rollers in the late eighteenth century; and a hundred years later Mace still found a market for the item. The form, a pine or walnut backboard with two projecting "ears" between which the free-turning roller was affixed, changed little with the passage of time. Winterthur Museum has a Pennsylvania example with scallop carved backboard. This is constructed in a similar manner to the spruce and black walnut rollers sold by Mace at anywhere from $1.00 to $3.50 a dozen depending on size and material.

## Hairpins

Wooden hairpins occasionally come to light. They are hand carved of hard wood and often enhanced with turned or gouge-cut decoration. Most seen in contemporary shops are European imports, so caution must be exercised in purchasing such pieces.

## Feather bed smoothers

Another bedroom item was the feather bed smoother, a flat paddle-shaped object twelve to eighteen inches long with a tapering handle and wide head. It was employed to smooth and flatten the bulky colonial feather bed after use and before storage. The smoother may be distinguished from a cooking or stirring paddle by its lack of wear and nontapering edge.

## Bed wrenches

For many years bedsteads lacked springs, and the mattresses lay on a nest of rope woven in and out of holes drilled in the frame. When the line slackened with use, it was tightened again with a wooden bed wrench or "key" (fig. 53). This was shaped like a giant clothespin, some fourteen inches long, with a crossbar at right angles. An unusual example at Sturbridge Village features a carved human head obviously inspired by the manlike form of the key.

## Chamber pots, bedpans, and cuspidors

While not likely to be much sought after, certain chamber "necessaries" were, on occasion, made of wood. In his *Treen and Other Wooden Bygones*, Edward Pinto describes a mahogany chamber pot with decorative incising, gilt paint, and the date 1871. The base of this vessel is inscribed: Presented by

Geo. A. Morse, January 1st, 1871. One can only speculate at the motivation behind such an unusual New Year's gift.

Turned wooden bedpans are also known. One circular specimen, a foot in diameter with a five-inch porringer-style handle, was made in two sections, a solid base and a removable donut-shaped top to facilitate emptying.

Cuspidors or spitting boxes were used in the home as well as in taverns, hotels, and most other public places. They were square with sides slanting outward toward the base, and frequently painted blue and filled with sand when in use. Both Isaac Ashton and David Evans of Philadelphia advertised cuspidors before 1800.

## Foot warmers

Another public necessity was the foot warmer. Few early public buildings, including churches, had any heating system, and winter travel was undertaken with a foot warmer for each person. The earliest were square wooden boxes, their sides punch-carved in geometric designs with stars, circles, and hearts predominating. A sliding door could be raised in order to admit the tin pan of hot coals. The examples shown in figure 53 are typical of this early form.

These warmers were very dangerous and after several Boston churches had burned owing to fires started by forgotten foot warmers, the municipal authorities, in 1768, levied a fine of ten shillings on absent-minded parishioners. Tin and iron warmers soon replaced their treen counterparts.

## Inkwells and sanders

Turned inkwells are often seen. The most common sort were intended to be used with a glass insert. The Silliman manufacturing company of Chester, Pennsylvania, manufactured such a well for over half a century, from 1820 until well into the 1880s.

## Woodenware 140

Sanders or sandboxes contained the sand that was sprinkled upon freshly inked surfaces to prevent smudging. They, too, were turned, often in an hourglass shape; and the fanciest were incised or made from two tones of wood. Representative forms of both inkwell and sander appear in figure 50.

### Pipe trays

The long-stemmed "Churchwarden" pipes favored by our forefathers were stored either in a wall rack or a pipe tray. The pipe tray was an elongated box divided into two long sections, with a smaller compartment at one end. The latter served as a receptacle for cleaning tools and similar accessories. There was often a handle affixed to the center divider. The wall rack shown in figure 67 has a drawer for tobacco beneath the open pipe storage area.

FIGURE 67 Left, *pipe wall rack;* right, *tinder box.*

## Snuffboxes and tinderboxes

Small, two- to four-inch, ovoid boxes, often of finely figured burl, were used to carry the snuff once popular with men and some women. The top might be turned to fit tight or be attached by a hinge at one side. They are a rare and interesting find.

Flint, steel, and singed cloth used in fire making were often kept in a tubular wood receptacle about four inches long. One or both ends were plugged with a cork or whittled plug. Countrymen favored wood over tin for this purpose as it neither rusted nor sank if lost overboard. In the house, a rectangular box (figure 67) with sliding top was employed to store such fire-making materials.

## Watch and seal boxes

The large pocket timepiece favored by prosperous burghers was stored for the night in a felt-lined painted wooden box. In Pennsylvania the multicolor ornamentation was floral and geometric; the traditional tulip was a popular motif. In other sections solid colors, black or black with gold trim, were traditional.

In the days when envelopes were closed with wax impressed with the initial seal of the sender, these seals were kept in small oval wooden boxes. The seal box was often formed from lignum vitae, burl, or some other rare wood.

## Comb cases, wig boxes, and cap stands

In Pennsylvania, combs were stored in a wall-hung comb box, a rectangular container frequently incised with geometric devices. Like all decorative boxes, these are much in demand for modern collections.

Wigs were also preserved in boxes. Samuel Matthews of

Philadelphia, though a cabinetmaker by trade, is known to have manufactured oval wig boxes during the late eighteenth century. They were generally stained black.

In the late nineteenth century, pressed wood cap-stands were popular with the ladies. They were made in two parts shaped roughly like an arrowhead and notched so that when locked together, they formed an X. A woman going on a visit carried the stand upon which she placed her bonnet cap for safekeeping while indoors.

## Bootjacks

Heavy boots and work shoes required a bootjack for removal. The earliest of these were rectangular wood blocks with a V cut in one end and a block nailed across the opposite end. The farmer placed the heel of one boot in the V cut and stood with his other foot on the blocked end of the jack. A stout knee lift removed the footgear. Later bootjacks were of cast iron molded in the shape of beetles, frogs, and the like. Several wooden jacks are pictured in figure 68.

*Figure 68.*

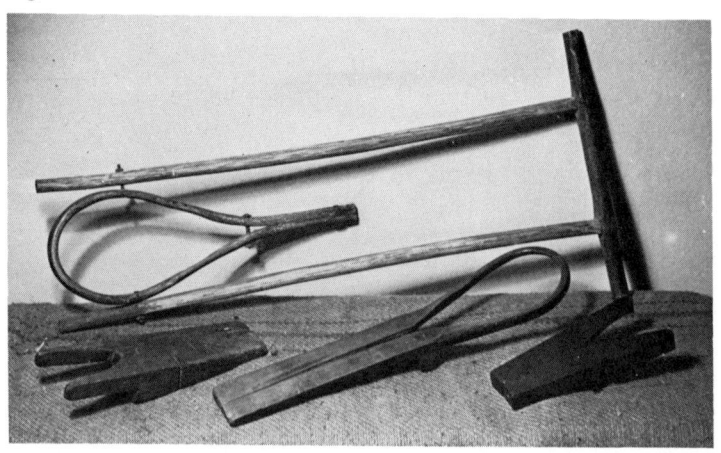

## Cane heads

Among the most unusual pieces of treen are carved cane heads. In an age of rheumatism, gout, and similar afflictions, most people beyond fifty used a cane at least part of the time. The ownership of a cane with a finely carved head or grip must have been a matter of some pride, for a wide variety have survived. Human and animal heads are the most common, and nearly all of these were hand carved. Presentation or gift canes may also bear names, dates, and even poems.

## Powder horns

Another elaborately carved type is the powder horn, which was a necessity in every frontier home from the sixteenth until the late nineteenth century. Pine or maple horns were inscribed with everything from names and dates to detailed maps or illustrations of famous battles.

## Lamp bases and candlesticks

Whale-oil lamp bases were occasionally made of treen that was ornately turned to duplicate the glass bases manufactured in volume by the Sandwich Glass Works and similar factories. Maple and burl wood were popular materials. An early worker in this line was Joseph H. Mather of Deep River, Connecticut, who offered both lamp bases and candlesticks in the 1830s.

Wooden candlesticks are still made. Like lamp bases, they are generally turned to imitate ornate examples made in other mediums, in this case pewter and bronze, though the simplest are nothing more than hollow tubes attached to a flat block base. Abner Taylor, of Lee, Massachusetts, had a rather substantial candlestick manufactory in the late eighteenth and early nineteenth centuries.

## Vases

Striped wood, produced by gluing together pieces of different-colored woods, then turning a form from the resultant block, was very popular in the late nineteenth century. Trays and pails were often made in this manner. Vases are less common. An unusual example with turned foot and tulip-shaped bowl is in the collection of Mrs. Raymond Delano of Nottingham, Pennsylvania. It is a "centennial item" commercially produced at the time of the 1876 centennial, and it bears on its base a label with shield and eagle and the manufacturer's mark: Ohl & Hanschild/Centennial Exhibition/Section C, 430 & 431/ Machinists, East Newark, N.J.

## Cribbage boards and checkerboards

Cribbage boards regularly appear in antique shops. They are of various woods and many were made from worn-out bread or chopping boards. A rare few have been decorated with incised geometrics, and these elicit most interest. They are invariably from Pennsylvania or Ohio. A very nice specimen in walnut is illustrated in figures 42 and 69.

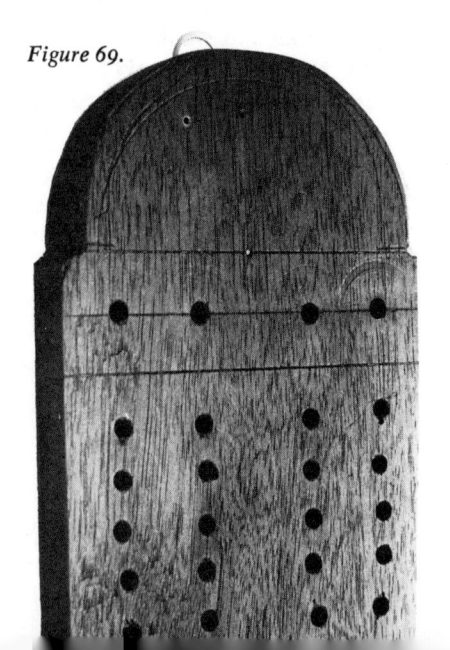

*Figure 69.*

Less common are homemade checkerboards. These are usually carefully hand painted, and originally were equipped with slices of nutshell or hand-whittled discs rather than factory-made checkers. The board shown in figure 50 is particularly well made.

## Medals and easter eggs

The introduction of steam-driven stamping machines led to a decline in carving. Under great pressure soft wood could be impressed with designs much in the same way a housewife might force cookie dough into a mold. Such items were the wooden medals, bearing likenesses of historic personages and buildings, that were manufactured for the 1876 Centennial by the Philadelphia Ornamental Wood Company.

But the old craft lingered on. Even in this century, obscure carvers in rural Pennsylvania were turning wooden easter eggs on a lathe, then scratch-carving them with decorative shapes unchanged for hundreds of years. The eggs were also colored red, blue, yellow, white, or in various combinations of these and sold locally. Since similar eggs have been imported from Poland and Czechoslovakia for some years, it is often difficult to distinguish the local product.

## Dishwashing tubs and dish strainers

Oval or round staved tubs, usually without handles (though some resembled large keelers), were used to do the after-meal dishes in most country homes. Being often in the water, they soon rotted out, and few are seen today.

One may also occasionally come upon a treen dish drainer made, in the shape of a crib or box, by joining turned rods and flat sticks. They were constructed in the pattern of Windsor furniture and look surprisingly like their modern plastic counterparts.

## Knife and pumice boxes

Another form still utilized is the knife board (fig. 54), which hung on the kitchen wall and was used for storage of various household edged implements. Slots in the horizontal portion of the board or rack kept the knives safely out of the way. Older examples show use scratches, and some have an attached sharpening stone, a feature rarely seen today. Two styles of such boards were sold by Mace: a long thin one and a shorter boxlike board with stone. Prices ranged from $2.25 a dozen for the "No. 1 Long" to $3.15 for the same quantity in "No. 2 Short."

Pumice boxes are flat trays with a boxlike compartment at one end in which was kept a piece of pumice, or "rotten stone," to scour knives with. The blades were laid on the long flat section of the tray and scrubbed until shiny with a mixture of pumice and water. Some of these boxes were hung on walls, while others were made with legs and sat directly on the sink or work bench. One of the footed specimens is illustrated in figure 54.

## Candle dippers and molds

Today, candle dippers or dips pass unnoticed by all but the most knowing. They are slim whittled sticks fifteen to eighteen inches long and often have shallow incised lines circling them at equal intervals. In the days when most people made their own candles, wicks were tied to these rods and dipped into hot wax over and over again until a tallow candle was formed. Candle molds replaced dipping, and most candle dips ended up in the kindling box.

Candle molds (fig. 70) were wooden frameworks housing from one to four dozen tin or pewter molds into which hot wax was poured. They replaced candle dips in the mid-nineteenth century.

FIGURE 70  Left, *candle mold;* right, *milking stool.*

## Flytraps

Perhaps the most bizarre of household woodenware is a rare spring-loaded flytrap. It was made in two sections, the upper portion being held open by the spring. Molasses was placed on the lower lip; then, after flies had gathered to eat the sweets, the housewife slammed down the lid, crushing them. The obvious impracticality of such a device aside, it is difficult to imagine a busy colonial dame skulking about the house waiting for pests to land in her trap.

## Brooms

Brooms have been made commercially for so many years that it is hard to imagine a time when they were created by hand. As recently as the 1870s, however, birch and beech were used in the manufacture of crude sweeping utensils. Least complex of these was the tool made by trimming a bunch of birch twigs and binding them to a rough branch handle with strips of bark or cord. Another, softer type was made by splintering the end of a birch rod into many fine fibers.

Such tools were used not only to sweep floors but to clean out ovens and large kettles, and, in smaller sizes, as egg and cream whips. Since the latter were difficult to clean, they were soon discarded, and early examples are uncommon.

### Candy scoops and buckets

Candy was sold to small storekeepers and to individuals in eight-sided buckets that were factory-made with mitered machine-dovetailed joinings. These receptacles had wire bail handles and flat covers with wooden lifts. The merchant also used wooden candy scoops that came in two standard sizes, one holding a nickel's worth of sweets, the other a penny's share. Tin and iron scoops were preferred for this purpose, and wooden specimens are unusual.

### Betty lamp stand

An extremely uncommon form in treen is the turned double stand intended as a support for iron "Betty Lamps." The base and shaft of the stand was formed from a single piece of treen. The wood had spiral grooves cut into it to receive an adjustable crossarm upon each end of which hung an iron lamp in the form of a flat dish. The lamps could be raised and lowered as needed.

### Storage buckets

Storage or utility buckets were a common sight in nineteenth-century homes. Sugar, flour, nuts, and other edibles as well as miscellaneous objects were stored in containers. Most often found is the sugar bucket. This is a staved receptacle one to two feet high, tapering slightly toward the top, and with a tight-fitting overlapping top similar to that used on a cheese box.

Top and bucket were made of pine, which transmits no odor or flavor to foodstuffs. Early examples were hooped with strips of thin wood while later factory-made types had narrow iron bindings. A loop handle of ash or hickory was secured to the body by means of wooden pegs driven through lift and body. The existence of such containers with hoops secured by copper staples indicates that the form was being made well into the twentieth century. Some later buckets have wire bail handles similar to those on candy buckets.

## Mousetraps

In 1883, L.H. Mace and Co. advertised three varieties of wooden mousetraps: a "common" in one to six holes, the "Delusion," and the "Wheel." The latter, which was intended (hopefully) to accommodate eight victims, was most expensive, selling for $2 a dozen. Single-entry traps were most common, and many were made both commercially and privately. Very often they amounted to nothing more than a hollowed-out wood block with a spring attachment intended either to drop a trap door or to propel a lethal metal shaft into the unsuspecting rodent. Such a crude example is shown in figure 46.

# Water-drawing and storage vessels

In the earliest days water was drawn from shallow wells in well buckets and stored in tubs and pails adjacent to the farmhouse kitchen. As time passed, the early wells were capped and fitted with wood, then later, metal pumps, while water coolers provided a more sanitary storage receptacle.

### Well buckets

The hand-drawn well bucket took a great deal of punishment as it was raised and lowered along the cobbled well shaft. Accordingly, these vessels were strongly made of thick oak staves bound with riveted metal. A heavy iron bale handle with rope loop was secured to rings driven into the sides of the bucket. Edmund Fuller of Hampton, Connecticut, manufactured receptacles of this nature in the 1880s, as did the Mace company. The latter advertised two capacities: "Light" and "No. 1," both hooped and handled in iron. The smaller version sold for $4.00 a dozen, the larger for $1.50 more.

So-called "suction buckets" had an iron trap door in the bottom attached with a metal or leather hinge. As the bucket was lowered into the water, the little door was forced open, causing the container to fill. Raising it caused the trap to close under pressure of the liquid within. Apparently, suction buckets were not popular, for few are found today.

### Water buckets

Well buckets were intended to be used and kept at the well mouth. The liquid was carried and stored in water buckets (fig. 71), and lighter pails. The former were frequently similar in construction to flour and sugar storage buckets. Both are made with staves and withe or iron hoops and loop handles. Water vessels, however, either are straight-sided or taper out from bottom to top, the reverse of the pattern in sugar buckets. Nor do the former have covers. Also, in water vessels the strap handle is attached to extended stave ears as in a maple sugar carrier rather than directly to the bucket sides. These protrusions enabled the bucket to stand clear of the ground when turned over to dry so air could circulate freely beneath it. Water buckets were made throughout the country, but few manufacturers specifically advertised them. An exception was Jacob Havens of French Creek, New York, who specialized in the item during the 1850s and 1860s.

The earliest buckets were put together by hand at the rate of half a dozen or so per day. Around 1825, Jehiel Wilson of Keene, New Hampshire, invented a form shaped like the exterior of a bucket upon which cut staves could be fastened. Then they would be swung over a lathe, which turned them to a uniform curvature. This innovation increased production by the hundreds and signaled the end of the era of the handmade bucket.

FIGURE 71   Left and center, *staved water buckets;* right, *canteen.*

## Water kegs, tubs, and coolers

Kegs holding several gallons were used to carry water on trips and into the fields. They were stave-constructed like barrels but smaller and usually narrower. Oak was the popular raw material, and the hoops and loop handle were of iron. Very often the bung hole in this form would be lined with pewter. The keg illustrated in figure 72 was designed to be carried horizontally.

Squat round tubs were produced in the second half of the nineteenth century for use as storage containers and to water stock. They had flat, machine-cut staves and were held together with thin tin bands. L.H. Mace and Co. offered such vessels in pine or cedar. The pine ones were left unfinished; the cedar were painted in blue or imitation oak grain. These receptacles were without handles or, at most, had a small wire lift loop at

FIGURE 72 Left to right, *small keg, canteen, handled water keg, rundlet.*

each side. Interestingly enough, Benjamin Thresher of Peacham, Vermont, is known to have made a similar tub up until the 1940s.

The problem of keeping drinking water fresh and tasty during the summer led to development of water coolers. In 1883, L.H. Mace sold ash coolers in three capacities; 12, 16, and 28 gallons. These were square boxlike affairs with a lift top into which liquid was poured and a pewter faucet at the base. Such receptacles were quite expensive. The three sizes offered by Mace cost $10, $13, and $16, respectively, at a time when many men did not earn even $10 in a week.

## Dippers and ladles

The traditional bucket companion has always been the dipper or ladle (fig. 48). As early as 1811, the Shaker turner Abiathas Babbit of New Lebanon, New York, was locally famous for his water dippers. The utensil varied in size from a foot or so in length to giants with handles as long as six feet and bowls holding up to three gallons. The form, however, was always pretty much the same, a handle with attached wooden bowl. In some cases, particularly with the choice burl dippers, both sections were turned from the same chunk of wood. Mace advertised such a form in 1883. Although it was called a ladle, the purpose and form did not differ. Small utensils of this nature were sold for ninety cents a dozen, while a larger size cost a dollar a dozen. In smaller communities craftsmen like Jacob Davis, of Sutton, New Hampshire, whittled all or part of each dipper by hand.

## Gourd dippers

Gourds grown to a suitable size and carefully dried were used as dippers, particularly in frontier areas. The hollowed-out vegetable was cut into two sections, the larger of which contained the gourd neck that served as a handle. In Pennsylvania and

Ohio gourd dippers were scratch-carved with designs of flowers and birds, then carefully painted in polychrome. Green, red, white, and brown were popular colors.

Authentic American dippers are rare in this medium, and the problem has been complicated by introduction of vaguely similar Mexican and African utensils.

# Butter-making implements

With the introduction of cows in the 1620s, milk and milk products became an important part of the limited colonial diet. Until the early twentieth century there were few rural New England families that could not boast of at least one cow; and only in recent years has the human population of Vermont come to exceed the bovine.

Little milk was drunk on the farm. Most of it was made directly into butter or cheese, the former being manufactured in a time-consuming though relatively simple operation, which required a few standard implements.

## Piggins and keelers

Milking was done with buckets or the bucketlike piggin, a staved and hooped hardwood vessel, eight to ten inches in diameter, with a single extended stave serving as a handle. This container was also used as a dipper and, no doubt, served other functions on the farm. The form is very old. A piggin valued at one shilling was among the items inventoried at the death of Richard Evered of Dedham, Massachusetts, in 1682. Purdon Keith of West Bridgewater, Massachusetts, was selling them for thirty-three cents each in the 1830s; and Jacob Davis and Son of Sutton, New Hampshire, carried the item until the late nineteenth century.

The day's accumulation of milk was poured into keelers, or keels, and placed in a cellar or springhouse to cool and to allow the cream in the milk to rise and separate. The keeler is a wide, shallow, round or oval, hooped tub. It has two protruding stave handles. An example appears in figure 45.

There were keelers in the estate of Daniel Fisher at Dedham,

Massachusetts, in 1683; and exactly two hundred years later, L.H. Mace and Co. offered seven varieties in pine or cedar, round or oval, painted or unfinished. The Mace vessels, however, were factory-made, bound with iron hoops rather than the wood or withe found in earlier examples, and with small iron loop handles instead of stave grips. They sold for eighty-five cents to seven dollars per nest of five.

### Skimmers and sour cream tubs

As cream formed on the surface of the milk, it was removed by use of an oval or shell-shaped skimmer. Skimmers are readily distinguished from dippers, ladles, and the like by their thin edge and lack of a handle. A skilled worker would use two at once, one in each hand. The cooper Timothy Gillette of Henniker, New Hampshire, made pine skimmers from 1817 until 1850.

Cream was stored in a covered bucket known as a sour cream tub until enough was accumulated to allow for churning. Examples known generally have wide staves, an inset lid, and a wooden bale handle, but any large bucket would suffice. The presence of residue left by years of cream storage is the real test.

### Churns

Churns, in which sour cream was converted to butter through agitation or "churning," were of many types. In all cases, the principle employed was the same. The cream was violently stirred in order that the outer skins of the oil globules therein would be broken. Once this occurred, the globules would adhere to each other as butter.

The earliest churn form was the tapering barrel-shaped vessel with a top through which a plunger with crossbars was inserted. Rapid up-and-down movement of this plunger provided the required agitation. In this form the motor power was

*Figure 73.*

entirely human; and, as noted by Samuel Deane in his *New England Farmer or Georgical Dictionary,* ". . . this work is very laborious, though it falls to the lot of the weaker sex most commonly to perform it." Churns in this primitive form were made throughout the United States and are still made. The small Gilland shop in Coleman, Texas, was making an oak version in 1880 that did not differ significantly from those advertised in the Mace catalog.

The arduous nature of the work involved led to numerous labor-saving churns. Among the earliest was the rocking churn, really nothing but a barrel lying horizontally on a pair of rockers, so it might be moved back and forth like a cradle. A later, modified form of rocking churn is illustrated in figure 73.

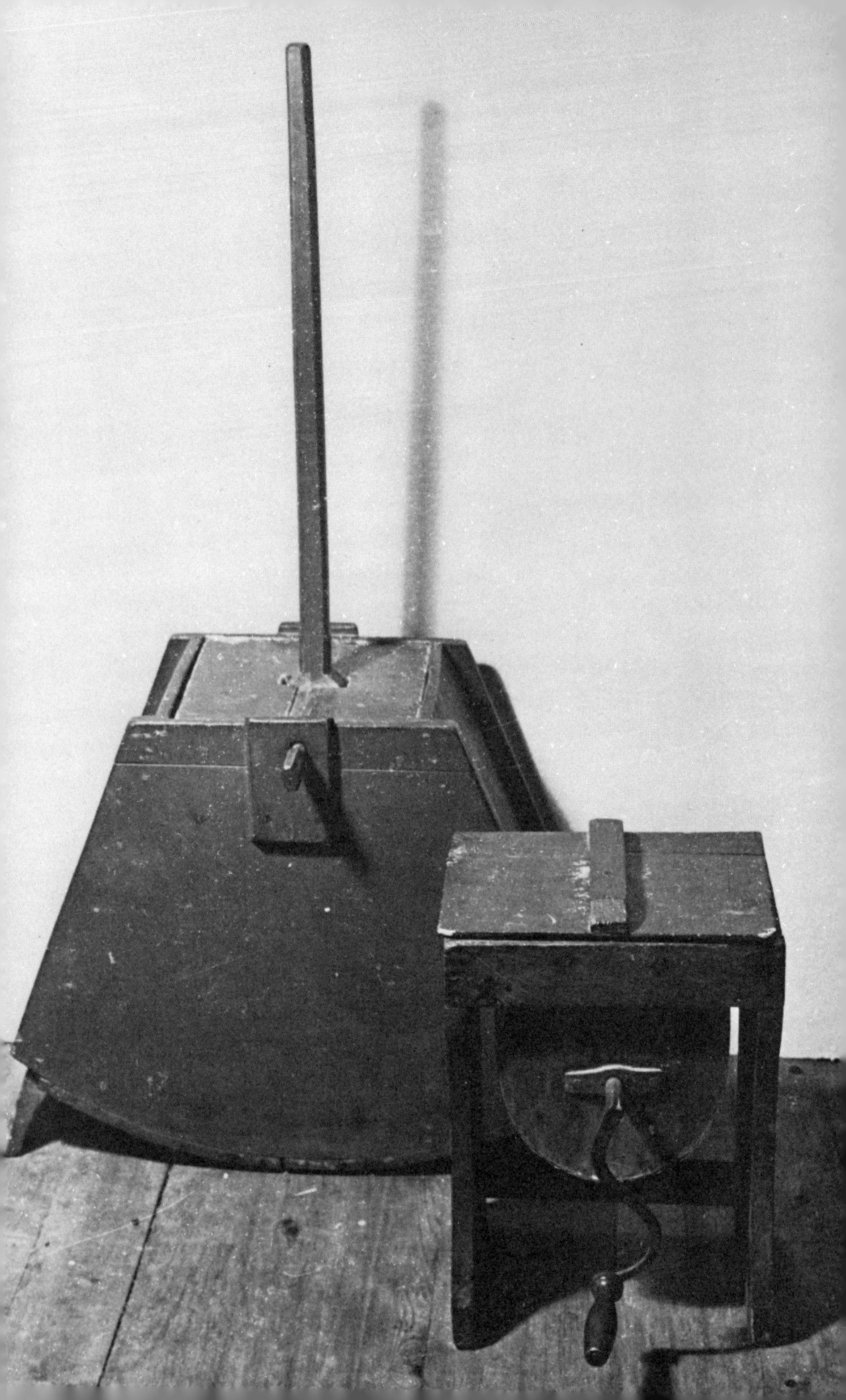

Many crank-driven devices were also patented, including the "Davis Swing Churn" made at Bellows Falls, Vermont, in the 1870s and 1880s. It consisted of a barrel resting on X-shaped cross supports with interior agitator paddles motivated by the turn of a hand crank. Similar examples (fig. 74), operate in the same manner but may have a fixed, boxlike form.

Somewhat different was the pump churn, where agitation was provided by the pumping of a water-well-type handle up and down. The square receptacle of this device even looks a bit like an early wooden water pump.

There was also a "wigwag" churn, where the dasher was fixed on a pivot so that instead of pumping it up and down, one needed only move it back and forth. An interesting "wigwag" churn from the Farmers' Museum collection is pictured in figure 74.

## Butter scoops, bowls, and paddles

Once the butter had "come," it was removed from the churn with long-handled wooden butter scoops and placed in a wooden bowl or tray, where it was kneaded and pressed with a butter paddle. This process served to remove water from the butter and to give it more body.

Butter paddles (fig. 30) are semicircular in form, with a wide flat handle providing a surface to place the hand on when working the butter. Mace advertised four varieties: "common," "half-size," "good," and "extra," ranging in price from $.75 to $1.15 per dozen. They were termed "butter ladles," a misnomer since the device was not used as a ladle or scoop but rather as a pressing tool.

Any bowl could and often did serve as a "butter bowl"; but generally a wide, shallow vessel such as that shown in figure 40, was preferred. Worked butter was often removed from the bowl with a bowl scraper, a piece of handled wood cut to fit the interior contour of the container.

FIGURE 74 (facing page)   Left, *Wigwag churn;* right, *barrel-type churn.*

A somewhat more specialized device was the butter worker, which was a fan-shaped tray with a low ridge on three sides. A smooth or corrugated rolling pin like rod with a handle at one end was rolled back and forth across fresh butter placed in the worker, thus smoothing it and removing excess water. While butter scoops, bowls, and paddles are quite common, a complete butter-working apparatus is seldom found.

### Butter tubs, tamps, and spades

Butter for storage or sale was packed either in bulk or in cut pound blocks. In either case it was stored in eighteen-inch-high staved and hooped tubs with close-fitting tops. Such a "butter tubb" was owned by Henry Wight of Dedham, Massachusetts, in 1681, and the firm of Ross, Gates and Smith at Bangor, New York, produced them in volume during the 1850s.

Where storage was in bulk, the raw butter was firmly packed into the container by use of a flat-headed wooden tamp, which looked much like an overgrown potato masher. One is shown in figure 40. For removal, a flat, narrow butter spade or spatula was employed. Two grades of these implements were sold by L.H. Mace and Co., at sixty-five cents and seventy-five cents a dozen. Two forms of butter spades are pictured in figures 40 and 30.

### Scales and testers

The marketing of butter led to the introduction of standardizing devices. All-wood butter scales, consisting of two square plates suspended by cord from an arm, were used to obtain exact weight, and hollow tubes a foot and a half long were used to obtain a cross section of butter packed in a tub. The latter device was necessary because rocks, wood blocks, and other foreign bodies as well as lower layers of rancid butter had a way of showing up in tubs of butter offered for sale.

## Scotch hands

Butter for table use was often, as today, rolled into little balls. Flat paddles with corrugated faces and short handles were used to produce these delicacies. One paddle was held in each hand, and a dab of butter was quickly rolled into shape between the ridged surfaces. These "Scotch hands" (fig. 30) should not be confused with the narrower spatulas and butter spades, since the latter were never corrugated.

## Butter prints and molds

The impressing of designs upon butter to make it more attractive for use and sale is an old American and European custom. The Palatine Germans of Pennsylvania are generally given credit for its introduction, though there can be no doubt that the practice was prevalent in New England at an early date. "Buttle Moles" were among the possessions of Nathaniel Draper of Roxbury, Massachusetts, at the time of his death in 1767.

Basically, the devices fall into two categories, prints and molds. The former were used to impress a design upon a block of butter. Mold-decorated butter was, on the other hand, forced into a hollow form and then removed bearing the mark of a pattern that had been cut into the interior of the mold. Both prints and molds appear in figure 75.

The typical print is a lathe-turned disc with or without handle, though cut square and rectangular examples are also known. The print face was decorated with a motif such as a cow, horse, star, or flower, either by hand carving or, at a later date, by machine-pressure stamping of steamed wood. In either case, the design was intaglio, i.e., it appeared in relief on the butter. The single stamp is most common, but variations are known. One example is a carved circular disc set within a handled frame so that it might be rolled across a piece of butter producing a band of decoration. Also, a form like rolling pin carved about its circumference with a multitude of figures was popular in New Jersey. It looked and worked like a cookie roller and produced a sheet of stamped butter that could then be cut into individually decorated squares. A sample of this roller is illustrated in figure 75.

FIGURE 75 *Butter molds, prints, and roller.*

Molds were of two basic types. The more common one consisted of a cup- or box-shaped form with a handled plunger. The motif was carved on the plunger face. Butter forced into the mold was impressed with this design, then forced out when the plunger was depressed. This form came in several standard capacities: one-sixth, one-eighth, one-quarter, one-half, and one pound. The box-shaped mold is pictured in figure 40.

Less often seen is the collapsible box mold, a rectangular hinged container with designs cut into one or more of the interior walls. Butter was tamped into this mold, which was then opened for removal by unhooking the hinged sides. A unique variety of box mold was six-sided and had removable set-in covers at each end. All surfaces were incised, so butter came from this mold in the form of a hexagonal column completely covered with decoration.

While few stamps or molds were marked by the maker, it is possible to generally identify certain ones as to area of origin. Those from Pennsylvania and Ohio tend to be very symmetrical, with a balanced design often consisting of a central figure such as a sheaf of wheat with a simple grain stalk incised on each side. New England examples, on the other hand, are often asymmetrical, with flowers or figures wandering aimlessly across the surface. Also, the western examples appear in a much greater variety with a multitude of flowers, animals, and human figures being known.

Some have said that molds were used as identifiers of marketed butter, with only one family in an area using a particular stamp. This may have been the case in some localities at an early period, but it is not likely to have persisted beyond the mid-nineteenth century. By then nearly all prints and molds were factory-made in standard designs. L.H. Mace and Co. sold a wide variety of each with prints costing from $.90 to $2.25 a dozen, and molds from $1.80 to $6.75, depending in each case on size.

# Cheese manufacture

Cheese making, once a nationwide occupation, is now confined primarily to commercial dairies in Wisconsin, New York, and Vermont. At one time, however, it was a vital task performed by nearly every rural household. Cheese will keep far longer than butter or raw milk, a major consideration in pre-refrigeration days. It is also a readily marketable commodity, which might be sold or bartered for things not available on the home farm. The process of manufacture is, however, a long and arduous one; and few families looked forward with any enthusiasm to the cheese making days of July and August.

## Curd knives and breakers

The first step in cheese making is curdling the milk or cream. Many years ago it was discovered that rennet, the dried stomach lining of young calves, contained an enzyme that would

FIGURE 76 Above left, *cheese basket and palette paddle;* above right, *curd breaker;* below right, *curd knife.*

curdle milk. Pieces of rennet dissolved in warm water produced a fluid, which was poured into containers of milk or cream. A long stick or spatula was used to stir the mixture until coagulation took place. The firm curds were cut and broken during the process with a long wooden shaft called a curd knife (fig. 76). As a more efficient alternative they might be ground in a curd breaker, which was a wooden box with interior teeth set on a shaft and turned by a hand crank. A well-made example of this device appears in figure 76.

## Cheese drainers and ladders

The raw curd was then placed in a cheese drainer in order to allow the whey, a clear straw-colored liquid that separates from the curd in the course of coagulation, to pass off. Cheese drainers are square or circular boxlike frames such as the one shown in figure 77. The earliest were, in fact, little more than boxes with drainage holes cut in sides and bottom. The later and more common examples are of rod construction, some as finely put together as Windsor chairs, whose turning they often imitated.

The interior of the drainer was covered with cheesecloth.

FIGURE 77 Left to right, *cheese ladder, cheese box, cheese drainer.*

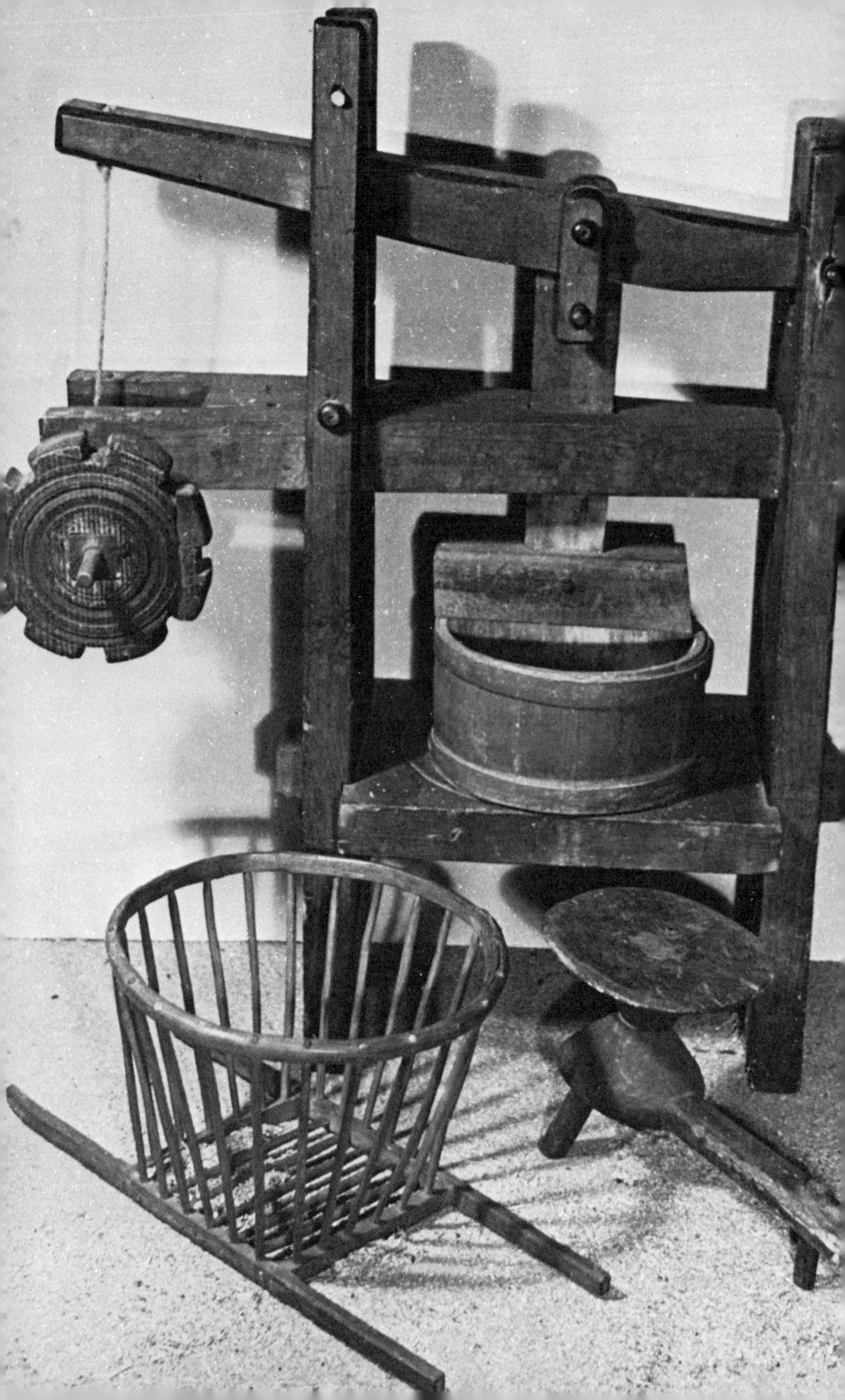

The curd mass was poured in while the drainer was on a cheese ladder over a tub into which the whey dripped. The cheese ladder (fig. 77) looked exactly like its larger counterpart, and the extended legs enabled the structure to fit securely over the drainage vessel. Quite often drainer and ladder were combined in a single piece, as in the work of Abner Taylor, a nineteenth-century cooper from Lee, Massachusetts. Such a combined unit is seen in figure 78.

The curd mass was next salted and worked to a fine consistency in a large wooden or earthenware bowl. A flat rectangular cheese worker (fig. 76) was employed for this purpose. Not all the whey had been removed at this stage, however, and final step was necessary.

## Cheese press, hoops, and follers

For this purpose and to compact the curd, a cheese press was employed. While the form varied, such presses are basically similar. The example illustrated in figure 78 worked like a pump. Two vertical and two horizontal boards were fixed in place, and on the lower or "baseboard," a circular groove with outlet spout was carved. In the upper horizontal a hole was cut through, which ran a vertical shaft attached by a movable bolt to a flexible upper arm. This third horizontal worked like a pump handle and could be lowered by tightening a cord joining its free end to a wooden wheel on the press frame. As the line became taut and the arm lowered, it forced down the attached plunger shaft.

Salted curd wrapped in cheesecloth was placed in a circular ash or hickory hoop (fig. 79) which looked much like a round box without top or bottom. The hoop was, in turn, placed on the baseboard and a loose-fitting cover of slightly smaller interior diameter called a foller was laid on top. As the cord tightened and the plunger bore down on the foller, the curd was forced into a compact circular mass while the whey flowed

FIGURE 78 (facing page)   Above, *cheese press with foller;* below left, *cheese drainer with attached ladder;* right, *milking stool.*

off by the outlet spout. In another type of press the shaft was driven down when a grooved wooden turn screw was cranked. Pressing could not be done all at once but required frequent tightening as the curd was compacted. Usually a full day of attention was necessary to complete the job.

Cheese presses appear frequently in the old inventories. One valued at two shillings was among the possessions of Richard Evered at Dedham, Massachusetts, in 1682 and another was in Ebenezer Jones' "Dairy room" when he died at Hingham in 1724. Less common are references to hoops, though three were owned by Enock Lovel of Weymouth in 1746. John Eaton of Jaffrey, New Hampshire, active in the 1770s, was one of the early cheese press manufacturers.

In New Mexico, goat milk cheese was made without benefit of a press on a flat table. The curd was kneaded by hand until compact, while the whey ran off the table through an incised lip. When ready, the curd was rolled and shaped into flat, circular cakes.

## Cheese boxes

After removal from the press, cheese was cured or seasoned for several months. During this period it was housed in the loose-woven splint cheese baskets described in the Basketry section. They allowed free circulation of air as did the tin- or cheesecloth-fronted cupboard in which they were stored.

For permanent storage or for marketing, cheese boxes were employed. These were flat, circular containers with close-fitting overlapping tops. The earliest were cut and joined by hand, and of ash or hickory wood that often was over a quarter-inch thick. Far more common are factory-made versions of thin veneer locked together with wire nails. They appear in a wide variety of sizes, reflecting the different preferences of cheese suppliers. They are often painted, and red, green, and blue are the most common tints. Examples of these appear in figures 77 and 35. Among the many manufacturers of cheese boxes were Payne Truman of Eaton, New York, active in the 1860s, and J.C. Brown of Painesville, Ohio, who worked well into the twentieth century.

# Apple preparation

Apples were the most important fruit available on eighteenth- and nineteenth-century farms. Dried or as cider, vinegar, applesauce, or apple butter, they provided much-needed vitamins and a welcome variation in the winter diet. In addition, hard cider was the most common alcoholic beverage available before 1800.

## Apple pickers

Apple orchards were planted in Massachusetts before 1650. In the next hundred years they spread over the New England states. Each fall the neighborhood gathered at one farm after another for a "picking bee," where dozens of hands quickly stripped one orchard after another.

The fruit was removed from lower areas of the tree by hand and from the upper branches with long-handled apple pickers. These were wooden rods with a series of springy prongs at the head. The picker head was fitted over an apple; then a quick twist freed the fruit, which was drawn safely to earth within the prongs. Several variations of pickers have been identified but all are scarce.

## Drying frames

One of the most common ways to preserve apples was drying. The fruit was sliced in quarters and placed on a drying basket (see Basketry section) or a wood drying rack. The latter was simply a rectangular framework with narrow slats nailed across it lengthwise. Apples were laid out on this frame in long rows and dried either outdoors in the sun or indoors in a loft or hanging from the ceiling before the fire. An interesting variation on the drying frame is pictured in figure 37. There, rough cut branches rather than slats are employed in the frame body.

## Apple butter stirrers and buckets, scoops

Dried apples were often converted to apple butter, popular both as a spread and as a sauce. The fruit was boiled in large brass or copper kettles (iron caused a black discoloration) and, while over the heat, was constantly worked with shovel-size stirrers. Since the quantities prepared were so large, some of these stirrers are five to nine feet in length. Typically, they had paddle-shaped heads, one to two feet long and a foot wide, set at right angles to the long handle. Holes drilled in the head reduced the friction as the stirrer moved through the thick mass.

Once prepared, apple butter was stored and transported in buckets. The Shakers sold a container for this purpose that was made of pine staves bound with iron bands, with a wire bail handle and set-in lid.

Large wooden scoops, some of them over a foot long, were used to handle bulk apple butter. They were relatively narrow and often had a square-eared handle with a cut-out finger grip, much like tin flour scoops.

Smaller utensils with a bowl-shaped head for dipping and a blunt end for stirring were used both for apple butter and applesauce. They are, appropriately enough, called "two-way scoops."

## Apple grinders

Cider, for many years the national beverage, was made each year in the early fall. Apples were allowed to fall and lie for a certain period until deemed ready. They were then bruised and crushed into pomace, a pulpy mass produced either by beating or by grinding in an apple grinder. The latter was a wooden box with an interior roller set with wooden teeth. Apples were placed in the grinder, the roller was turned by a crank, and the fruit was reduced to a suitable consistency.

### Cider press racks and pomace rakes

The ground fruit was then laid on a square wooden framework with narrow slats. Layers of pomace were alternated with layers of straw to build up a "cheese" on this cider press rack (fig. 15). At a later date the pomace was simply placed in burlap bags with racks separating each bag. Some cider presses and racks were so large that wooden-toothed spreaders called pomace rakes were used to spread the mash evenly.

Press racks are rare today but many must have once existed. There was one in the possession of Nathaniel Draper at Roxbury, Massachusetts, in 1767, and many others were made in the eighteenth and nineteenth centuries.

The racks of pomace were placed in a cider press that was either manual or steam-driven. In the former, a large wooden screw was ground down to crush the pomace, forcing the cider to run out through the slats in the rack while the dried pomace was squeezed out the sides of the press. In the latter, the same result was obtained by application of mechanical means.

### Cider "cheese" cutters

In the days of hand presses, a cider "cheese" cutter was employed to cut up and remove the compacted mash and straw following pressing. This was a wooden shovel with a pie-slice-shaped blade. It was some four feet long and often had a square-eared handle. The blade edge was cut to a sharp angle so that it could be used to scoop up the sticky residue.

## Cider barrels and funnels

Buckets and tubs below the press caught the dripping cider, which was then removed to large barrels for storage. Staved and hooped barrels, first made by hand and after 1850 by machine, were an important cooper's ware. Because they contained liquids, they deteriorated rapidly, so new ones were in constant demand. The average cider barrel held from five to fifteen gallons. One of the largest late-nineteenth-century manufacturers was the Oakland Box and Barrel Company of Oakland, California.

Cider was transferred to the barrels with a cider funnel, a staved vessel as large as a bucket and constructed similarly, with a wooden aperture six inches long and two inches in diameter. In some cases, these funnels were used to channel the flow of fresh cider from the press into catchment tubs.

FIGURE 79  Above left, *shoulder yoke for sap carriers;* right, *maple sugar bucket;* below, *spiles used in gathering maple sap.*

# Maple sugar equipment

It was well into the nineteenth century before commercial cane sugar became available in the average household. Until that time, particularly in rural northeastern areas, the common sweetener was maple sugar. Even today maple syrup and sugar candies are much in demand. The techniques employed in refining these products have changed little with the passing years.

### Syrup spiles, troughs, and buckets

In the early spring, when the warming weather caused sap to begin to travel up the capillary system of maple trees, holes were bored into the bark with an auger or brace and bit, and into these were driven hollow wooden tubes or spiles (fig. 79), a few inches long. Sap flowed out along these spouts and into collecting vessels. James and Johnson, in their *Remarks on the Manufacturing of Maple Sugar*, described the use, in 1790, of maple syrup "troughs," crudely hollowed sections of pine or ash trunk with a two- or three-gallon capacity. These were placed on the ground beneath the spile, and the sap dripped into them.

A more efficient device was the sap bucket, a staved and hooped vessel with a single protruding handle containing a hole by which it was hooked over the spile. The collecting vessel thus hung on the tree directly below the source of sap rather than several feet below.

Sap buckets are somewhat similar to piggins but may be distinguished from the latter in that the bucket is made to taper from the bottom up, while piggins are straight-sided. Also, the former always has a drilled hole in the stave handle. A well-made sap bucket is pictured in figure 79.

Such containers were commercially made throughout the nineteenth century. In the 1850s the Niagara Pail and Tub Factory at Buffalo, New York sold unpainted pine sap buckets for only $16.00 per hundred. At the same time, in the tiny community of Walton, New York, Henry Eells informed the public that he "is prepared to supply them with a first rate article of Sap Buckets, hooped with iron, and painted outside." He further noted that "those wishing any, will please leave their orders as soon as possible, that he may have them on hand in season."

### Sap carriers and shoulder yokes

Similarly tapered buckets having two short stave ears were employed to transport sap from the tree to the sugar house. When the collecting bucket became full, its contents were poured into a carrier. A wooden rod or dowel was inserted through holes drilled in the carrier ears and hooked thongs of a shoulder yoke secured to the rod.

This yoke, an example of which is seen in figure 79, was a section of hand-carved wood about three feet long hollowed out to fit comfortably about the neck and shoulders and tapering to blunt ends. From each extremity hung a thong terminating, as mentioned, in an iron or whittled wooden hook. Since sap carriers were more or less of a standard size, they balanced neatly, one on each side. To prevent slippage, the carrier rods were grooved in the center to receive the hooks. Yokes were also used to carry milk and appear quite frequently in shops and at shows.

### Maple scoops and molds

The collected sap was boiled down to syrup in large iron kettles whose contents were constantly stirred with giant scoops or spoons (fig. 47). Gould describes one of these now rare implements as being over three feet long with a head seven inches in depth. They look much like bread peels and may be confused with the latter.

The clearer "first run" of syrup was poured into molds to harden and crystalize. The standard form was a large box divided into pound-capacity squares by removable partitions. Once the sugar had hardened sufficiently, the partitions were removed, leaving a dozen or so individual pieces.

More interesting are the decorated molds, usually individual blocks a few inches across with an incised design on the bottom, much like a butter mold. Maple sugar candy is still made in such molds or in multiple versions, where the sugar cubes are cut apart like cookies after they harden. Sugar molds were never made in the variety of motifs used for butter molds. Simple patterns such as stars, flowers, and pine trees were typical, and most were machine-made.

### Sugar storage tubs

Maple sugar was stored in large staved tubs with a close-fitting overlapping lid. Some of these vessels were three feet high and eighteen inches across the mouth. They were made tight to prevent entry of insects and rodents. Individually wrapped pieces of cake or block sugar were neatly stacked in their interiors to provide a year's sweets. Soft sugar, a darker, coarser confection made from the last run of sap, was also stored in sugar tubs, but in this case a small hole was drilled at the tub base. The sugar was put away damp, and a fluid called sugar molasses was collected in the lower portion of the tub, from which it was periodically removed by uncorking the bung hole. Both forms of sugar were commonly stored in a dry attic or loft to avoid mold damage.

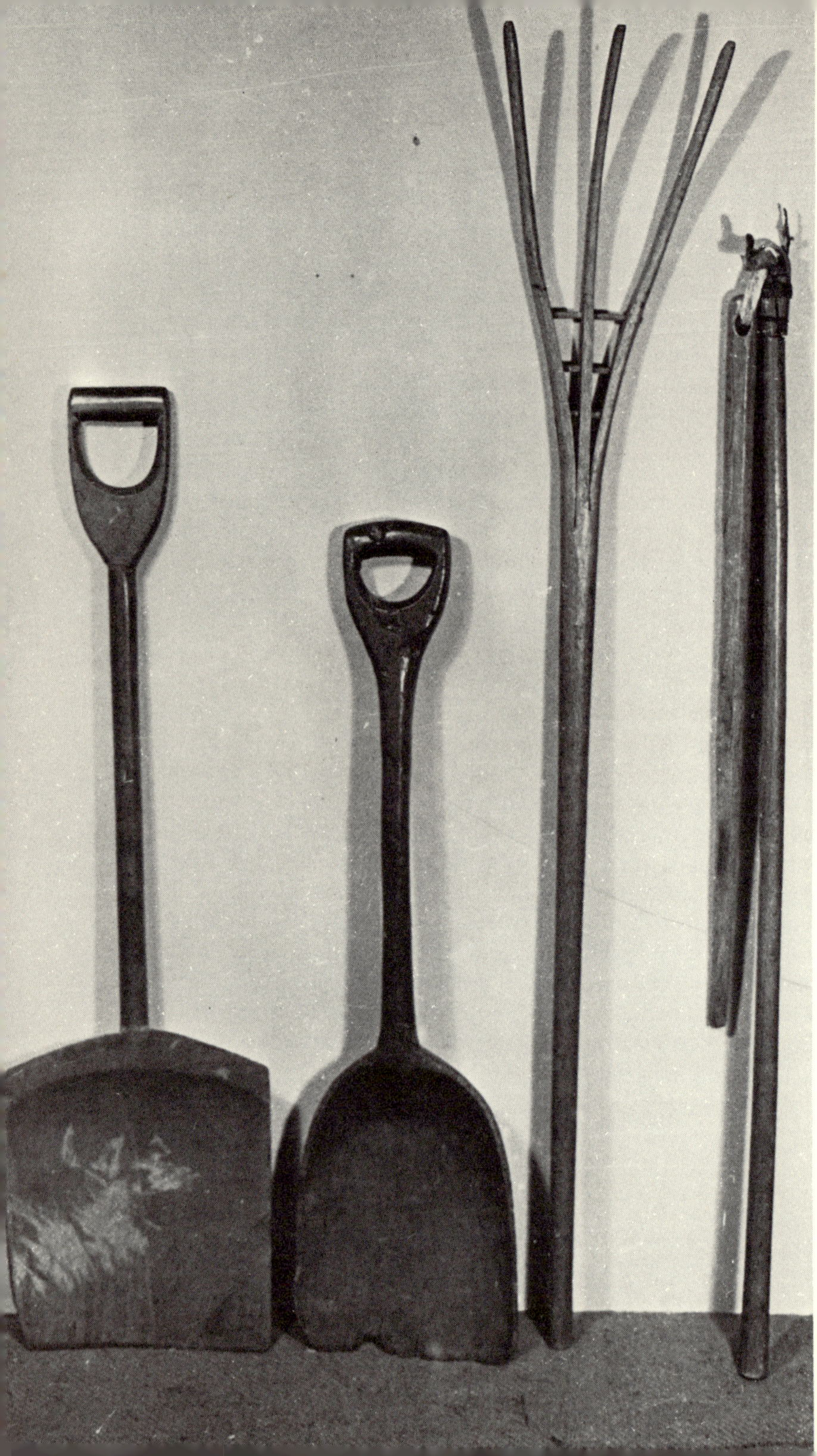

# Wooden farm implements

Treen was a most important material on the early farm. It was readily available when iron was scarce and expensive. Even after the latter became popular, wood continued to be preferred for many jobs, most notably haying and produce handling. While hickory, pine, and maple were favored, a wide variety of trees provided raw material for the agricultural craftsman.

## Mallets and mauls

Perhaps the most common wooden tools were mallets and mauls. The first were square or round hardwood heads, about three inches across with an attached wooden handle. In the case of burl mallets, which were greatly favored because of their exceptional strength, the burl growth might form the mallet head and an adhering branch, the handle. In the 1880s, L.H. Mace and Co., of New York, sold four different mallet types including two sizes in lignum vitae at $3.00 and $5.00 per dozen and a large iron-bound hickory example at $6.50 for twelve.

Mauls were a much larger version of the same utensil, with a handle nearly four feet long and a head eight inches across. They too were often headed in burl and were used to drive fence posts.

## Shovels, rakes, and forks

Until well into the nineteenth century, farm shovels were commonly made of wood. Grain shovels (fig. 80) with deep ovoid

FIGURE 80 Left to right, 1–2, *grain shovels*, 3, *hay fork*, 4, *flail*.

bowls and long-eared handles were used to carry apples and various grains. The wood, unlike metal, did not bruise the produce. Also, wooden shovels were much lighter than their iron counterparts, an important factor in the backbreaking daily labor. Maple and poplar were most often used for these implements, and a rare burl example is known.

Wooden snow shovels persisted into this century; and square-bladed examples with metal-tipped lips and turned handles regularly appear in country shops. Mace stocked them in 1883, offering large wooden ones for $4 per dozen. Nearly two hundred years previously, such a "shod shovel" was in the estate of Dr. Jonathan Avery, who died at Dedham, Massachusetts, in 1691.

Rakes and forks were often made entirely of wood. The former consisted of a rectangular block about eighteen inches long and three inches wide into which short dowels were set, all in a row. A long whittled or turned handle completed the implement. The largest of these was the "Bull Rake," or hay drag, which was often five feet across the base.

Forks are perhaps the most graceful of all farming treen. The earliest are nothing more than naturally pronged branches, trimmed and shaped. Later four- or six-tined examples were made by squaring an ash or hickory limb, shaving down the shaft and carefully splitting it into equal portions, which would then be blocked to keep them splayed. This method of manufacture is evident in the example shown in figure 80. These hay forks, some of them nearly three feet across the basket, have a grace and form that is seldom seen in later implements.

An interesting variation is the three-tined barley fork, which had a fourth thumblike tine set in directly opposite the others in order to better grip its load during transfer from field to wagon or wagon to barn.

Potato forks or diggers were similar in outline to a spade fork, with a series of wooden teeth braced by crosspieces and secured to a long handle with a turned or carved grip.

## Hay crooks

A rarely seen implement once common in the hayfield is the hay or grass crook. This was a yard-long rod with fishhook-shaped head which was used to grasp patches of grain or grass and pull them forward to be cut by the sickle. It was also used to pull hay out of a closely packed stack.

## Flails

For generations, one of the hottest, dustiest rural jobs was flailing grain. A long wooden handle and a shorter piece, perhaps two feet long, were joined by a leather strap or, in later models, by a ball and swivel. Grain from the fields was spread on a barn floor and beaten with flails swung in a rhythmic pattern, thus separating kernels from chaff.

The handle portion of the flail was termed a staff and the shorter section, a swingle or swiple. The flail illustrated in figure 80 is typical. Many thousands must have been made, for despite hard usage, large numbers remain.

## Winnowing scoops

After being beaten with flails, grain was separated from chaff by being thrown in the air from a winnowing scoop. The wind would blow away the lighter debris, and a talented winnower could catch most of the grain in the scoop as it fell.

Scoops were semicircular, three to four feet across the mouth, and had a ridge running about the sides and rear. Bent ash handles on each side were gripped by the worker as he flung the grain into the air. Though made of hickory or another durable wood, winnowing scoops were often damaged when beaten on the floor to loosen chaff clinging to the frame. As a result, they are seldom seen today.

## Husking pins

Corn harvesting was facilitated through use of a husking pin, a sharpened wooden peg three to five inches long with an attached thumb strap. Worn on the hand, it facilitated the tearing open of cornhusks.

## Corn-shelling tubs and graters

Removing kernels of corn from the cob was even more difficult than removing the husks from the cobs. At first the dried meats were pounded off with a yard-long wooden pestle. For this purpose the cobs were dumped into a corn sheller, which was a hollow log with holes drilled in the bottom or a grating of iron rods. As they were dislodged, the kernels fell through the openings into a waiting tub or basket. An example of this crude device appears in figure 81.

*Figure 81.*

# Wooden farm implements 183

Somewhat less tiring to use was a hand corn sheller. This consisted of a chairback platform upon which is affixed, by means of a swivel, a paddle-shaped board. The facing surfaces of both platform and paddle are lined with iron nails, forming a coarse grater. Ears of corn are forced between the two nail beds and ground back and forth through movement of the paddle, thus breaking off the kernels.

## Palette paddles

In time, all grain came to be ground at a commercial mill. Here it was shoveled with wooden shovels and lifted out of the mill box with palette paddles, rectangular pine boards with thumb and finger holes which were worn as boxlike extensors by the mill hands. These paddles are seldom seen or recognized today.

## Grain measures

Both miller and farmer were concerned with a correct messure; and for this purpose, they used carefully standardized receptacles. These grain measures ranged in capacity from one to sixteen quarts and were sturdily made of quarter-inch hickory nailed together with square-headed nails and reinforced by thin metal bands that ran down the sides and across the set-in bottom. Such "iron bound" varieties sold for fifty cents more per dozen than their unshod cousins. A classic example may be seen in figure 61 and is dated 1832.

Measures were often dated and bore, on occasion, the name or initials of a local official whose duty it was to verify the correctness of measuring devices. An interesting example illustrated in the February 1935 issue of *American Collector* had been made in too-large capacity, so a block of wood was inserted, stamped with the name of the local sealer of weights and measures, to verify the change.

Measures were sold in nests of five at one, two, four, eight, and sixteen quarts. Also, corn was measured in four-bushel containers called coombs.

Grain measures were manufactured all through the country. In the East, Mace stocked them throughout the 1880s, while in upstate New York, Jacob Phillips of Northampton is known to have made the item during the 1850s. Generations before, Henry Wight of Dedham, Massachusetts, had, at his death in 1681, "a bushel measure . . . a halfe bushel and halfe peck measures." The bushel was valued at two shillings, sixpence; the others at only two shillings for both.

## Feedboxes

Wooden feedboxes and troughs in many shapes and sizes were and are still common in the barn and outbuildings. The first of these were hollow logs or split trunks gouged into shape.

In the 1850s, L.T. Kinney, a Vermont turner from Marshfield, sold the outer shells of wood blocks from which bowls were cut as pig troughs—a notable example of Yankee ingenuity.

Later troughs are rough box forms, sometimes with hinged lids so that they might be lowered to keep rodents out of the feed while the farm animals were not in their stalls.

## Kits and herb trays

Smaller wooden vessels served other purposes. Butter, fish, and no doubt other materials were carried in machine-made staved pails bound with thin iron hoops. These were made to taper in from top to bottom to provide stability and were generally no more than two quarts in capacity.

Much more graceful is the herb tray, an oval, shallow-sided receptacle with a flat, bent wood handle arching across its middle. Gould describes one fully two feet long and nearly eighteen inches in width. Herb trays were used to bring picked condiments and medicinals in from the fields. They were lightly made to carry easily across a woman's arm and were not intended to bear heavy loads.

## Clam rollers

Quite a different thing was the clam basket or roller, though it too had an arching handle and oblong shape. This boxlike structure was made by nailing slats to end boards and adding a pine branch handle. Its purpose was to carry clams or oysters, and the slatted design allowed excess water to pass off, thus lightening the bearer's load.

## Bee finder's and pigeon boxes

Two rare farm box forms are the bee finder's box and the portable pigeon box. The bee box (fig. 46) was used in searching for wild honey. It was a rectangular container approximately one foot long and four inches square. A sliding lid covered the top and in this was a wire-screened window. Bee hunters would go into the fields, catch several bees, and place them in the box, which contained honey. After the bees had had an opportunity to collect some of the sweet substance, they were released and followed as they carried it to their hive. Not a nice trick, but effective.

The portable pigeon box was a forerunner of today's skeet or trap devices. In the days when it was legal to kill pigeons in any number and at any time, giant pigeon shoots were held, where thousands of the live targets were slaughtered with prizes awarded to the best marksmen. The pigeon box was designed to release a live pigeon so that it might fly before the waiting shooters. The box, about ten inches by fourteen inches and eight inches high, was made in three sections, a base and two hinged sides, spring-loaded, so that they would pop open when a locking pin was pulled. Each box held only a single bird, so hundreds must have been used at some contests. Yet, very few examples remain.

## Yokes and pokes

In the days prior to the era of modern transportation, loads were drawn by an amazing variety of animals. Best known, of course, is the ox, and ox yokes are widely collected often ending up as a chandelier or mantel decoration. This form of yoke is shaped roughly like a pair of old spectacles, with the hoops that went about the animals' necks corresponding to the lower

*Figure 82.*

glass rims, as may be seen from figure 82. The massive yoke body, often five feet across, was first carved from pine or oak. Later, the wood was steamed and forced, while flexible, into a mold of the appropriate shape. Pins were inserted to hold this form, and the piece was then allowed to season. So large were these yokes that the mold was carved from a tree trunk. The two hoops, one for each animal in the pair, were also steamed and forced into an appropriate curve, then set into the bow body through drilled holes. There were five "oxe yoakes" in the estate of Dedham's John Farrington in 1676. In Texas,

Joseph Jackson and his sons, at Lexington, made a high-quality ox yoke from 1840 until well into this century.

Children's carts and wagons were often pulled by geese or turkeys. The former were secured with a yoke identical in form to, but much smaller than, an ox yoke. The average goose yoke is about sixteen inches in length. Turkey yokes are much less common and are differently made. They are usually a single piece of light wood shaped to a dumbbell form with each end hollowed out like a donut. Goats, when used as beasts of burden, were served with single yokes of the form shown in figure 83.

Pokes also went about an animal's neck but served a different purpose, as they were intended to prevent its jumping through fences. There were two kinds. The first was a anchor-shaped wooden block with rods set in each side, which hung from a cow's or horse's neck and was intended to tangle in wire fencing. A different principle was embodied in the frame poke (fig. 83). For geese it was a Y-shaped branch end with a removable rod that fit across the wide part of the frame. This was placed over the goose's head and kept it from getting through barriers. For cows, a rectangular frame some four feet long served the same function.

FIGURE 83 Above, *single ox yoke;* below, *goose yoke.*

## Ox drag shoes

The ruggle, or ox drag shoe, was also intended to slow an animal's progress but for a much different purpose. A ruggle, which looked something like a toy boat with no stern, was placed beneath each rear wheel of a heavy wagon when it was going downhill in order that the vehicle would not overtake the oxen or horses that were pulling it.

## Gambrels and hooks

Gambrels, or hog stretchers, and hanging hooks were among other miscellaneous agricultural treen. The former was a yard-long wooden rod, slightly curved and with a short cross rod set in near each extremity. After butchering, hog carcasses were spread apart with gambrels so that they might drain and cool.

Hooks, formed in a V shape by trimming a tree branch, were common features of rural barns well into the twentieth century. They were nailed to a beam or rafter and served to support everything from harness to washtubs.

## Sheep and bag stamps

In order to identify their animals and their grain, the settlers devised wooden stamps bearing numbers, initials, or fanciful designs. Least complex are individual hand-carved numerals used to mark sheep turned out into common pasture. Ochre or lamp black mixed with grease provided the pigment.

While he might identify his animals by number, the farmer generally marked the bags of grain sent to market to be milled with an ornate wood block carved to contain his initials or full name and surrounding decorative devices. In Pennsylvania and New Jersey, these were often quite elaborate, with geometric patterns being favored.

## Blueberry and cranberry scoops

Blueberries and cranberries are both low-growing plants necessitating tiring stoop labor to harvest them. The scoop was devised to ease this chore. It is an open-ended box with the lower edge of the open end cut into parallel teeth. A handle is affixed opposite the toothed portion. The worker pushes the scoop gently through the bushes. The berries are caught in the teeth and removed from the vine, falling into a rear storage area.

Cranberry scoops differ from blueberry scoops or rakes only in being larger and in usually having two handles rather than one. Both implements are still used in the berry harvest, though modern examples are metal rather than wood.

## Grease buckets

A common sight hanging at the side of early wagons was the grease bucket. This vessel, made from a hollowed-out log about two feet deep, was bound with iron bands and had a set-in cover. The wooden lid had protruding ears through which ran a carrying line, as well as a large center hole. A stick was dipped into the bucket through this hole and tar or pitch removed to grease the vehicle's axles.

## Canteens, kegs, and rundlets

Canteens, specimens of which are shown in figures 71 and 72, were a common necessity among field workers; many once existed, though they are now rare. The basic form is circular, not unlike a very shallow round box but without a removable cover. Instead, the canteen has a bung hole, a small drilled aperture in one side by which the vessel is filled and emptied. Unlike kegs and barrels, canteens are not staved but rather made from veneer that is lapped over and nailed tight. Many early examples were caulked like a boat to prevent leakage.

Water and rum were the usual contents, though a "beer cag" is mentioned among the assets of Samuel Gardner at Brookline, Massachusetts, in 1771.

Kegs, figure 72, are much more like narrow barrels. They are staved and hooped either with wooden or iron bands and have a bung hole in the head and another midway along the body. Oak is a popular material because it is durable and resistant to rot. A keg was typically one and a half to two feet high and up to a foot across at the widest spot.

While most kegs had the bulged form of a barrel, rum kegs were made with incurved staves supposedly so they might more readily be carried under the tippler's arm.

The rundlet (fig. 72) was a keg in different form, as it was triangular rather than round in cross section. Originally, rundlets were intended to hold eighteen gallons, but the term came to apply to any triangular keg regardless of capacity. The form is quite old, and the vessels appear frequently in ancient inventories such as that of Thomas Jones, who died at Hingham, Massachusetts, in 1724.

Another variation is the oyster keg, a crudely made vessel with a hole several inches across in the top. Oysters were inserted and withdrawn through this opening. These kegs were filled, then packed in ice and shipped surprisingly long distances to satisfy the demands of oyster houses throughout the Middle Atlantic states.

### Swiglers

Tiny cylindrical kegs, no more than half a foot tall, were known as "swiglers." One appears in figure 72. They were sometimes made of staves in the same manner as their larger cousins. Others were formed from a hollow piece of wood with a head set in at each end. Whiskey, principally rum, was carried in these containers. They were also copied in redware and stoneware; and examples in these media are extremely rare.

## Whetstone holders

Every farmer used a sickle or the long-handled scythe, and both implements were quickly dulled through contact with rocks and sticks in the hayfield. For sharpening these blades, a whetstone was carried hanging from the worker's belt in a hollow wooden cone. The holder was eight to ten inches long and was, on occasion, incised with the owner's name or initials.

## Milking stools

A variety of squat, easily carried stools were used for milking. Interesting early examples may be carved from a single block of wood (fig. 70) or, more often, several pieces pegged together. They generally had three legs and some had swivel seats. The one illustrated in figure 78 is very old and of an uncommon form.

## Samp mortars

In all recently settled areas, prior to the building of mills, grain was ground in a primitive samp mortar made from a hollow tree trunk often four feet high and a yard wide. This mortar was set up, outdoors, adjacent to a small supple tree, to the trunk of which was attached a large stone or wooden pestle. After the pestle was driven down into the mortar, the spring of the tree would lift it out again thus reducing somewhat the tiring work involved. Such mortars were also known as sweep mills and were used primarily to mill corn and wheat. Few exist today.

# Appendix: A List of Early American Basket and Woodenware Makers

The following listing of American basketry and woodenware manufacturers is intended as a guide to assist collectors in researching the backgrounds of such artisans as are known to have worked in their states. It is not all-inclusive, as thousands of people worked in these crafts, many of whom never advertised or did anything else to bring themselves to the attention of the researcher.

The serious collector, however, should be able through examination of early local newspapers, directories, and histories to add to this appendix as it applies to the locality he or she is interested in.

| City | Company | Year | Item |
|---|---|---|---|
| **CALIFORNIA** | | | |
| Oakland | Oakland Box & Barrel Company | ca. 1887–90 | Boxes, barrels |
| San Francisco | Walter Moses & Co. | ca. 1877–78 | Baskets |
| | John Robinson | ca. 1877–79 | Willowware |
| | F. Tewes | ca. 1877–78 | Willowware |
| | Victor Navlet | ca. 1860–78 | Baskets |
| | Armes & Dallam | ca. 1859–92 | Pails, Tubs, Washtubs |
| | Pacific Woodenware Co. | ca. 1878–91 | Pails, Boxes |
| | San Francisco Planing & Sawing Co. | ca. 1856–57 | Fruit Boxes |

| City | Company | Year | Item |
|---|---|---|---|
| | Hobbs, Gilmore & Co. | ca. 1854–60 | Boxes |
| | J. & B. Johnson | ca. 1868 | Bonnet Boxes |
| | William Becker | ca. 1872–82 | Willow Baskets |
| | Paul Lindemann | ca. 1872 | Baskets |
| | Elam & Howes | ca. 1868–72 | Tubs, Pails, Washboards |
| | Chris Hennes & Co. | ca. 1878 | Willow & Rattan Baskets |
| | Mariana Gagliardi | ca. 1882 | Baskets |
| Sacramento | Bockera Brothers | ca. 1873–75 | Willowware |
| **CONNECTICUT** | | | |
| Bridgefield | Jared St. John | ca. 1866–68 | Butter Tubs |
| Canterbury | Norman Park | ca. 1865–70 | Rakes |
| Chester | The Silliman Co. | ca. 1820–80 | Inkwells |
| Danielson | Joseph Codding | ca. 1868–84 | Wagon, Cheese, Clam, Market & Coal Baskets |
| Deep River | Joseph Mather | ca. 1830–32 | Lamps & Candle Sticks |
| Fairhaven | Richard Schofield | ca. 1866–69 | Baskets |
| Hampton | Edmund Fuller | ca. 1880–85 | Buckets, Barrels |
| Hartford | John Donovon | ca. 1866–68 | Woodenware |
| | Colts' Willow Ware Co. | ca. 1866 | Willowware |
| Killingly | R.N. Potter & Co. | ca. 1867–71 | Bobbins |
| Killington | Nathan Lane | ca. 1864–66 | Ox Yokes |
| New Britain | American Basket Co. | ca. 1869–72 | Fruit Baskets |

| City | Company | Year | Item |
|---|---|---|---|
| New Haven | David Cook | ca. 1859–64 | Fruit Baskets |
| | Robert Bradley & Co. | ca. 1866–70 | Woodenware |
| | R.C. Dickinson & Co. | ca. 1865–67 | Woodenware |
| | Smith & Stevens | ca. 1866–70 | Flour Sifters |
| Northford | Malby, Fowler & Co. | ca. 1831–35 | Shaving Boxes, Spoons |
| Plymouth | E. R. Ives & Co. | ca. 1866–70 | Baskets |
| Robertsville | Lyman Benedict | ca. 1866 | Cheese Boxes |
| Southington | Bills & Gleason | ca. 1865–70 | Churns |
| Stamford | Harry Taylor | ca. 1865–66 | General Woodenware |
| Westville | Beecher Basket Co. | ca. 1864–78 | Fruit Baskets |

## DELAWARE

| City | Company | Year | Item |
|---|---|---|---|
| Ashland | B. McCanns | ca. 1890–93 | Brooms |
| Farmington | P. Prettyman | ca. 1890–92 | Baskets |
| Felton | Hubbard & Sons | ca. 1889–91 | Baskets |
| Laurel | Adams & Co. | ca. 1890–92 | Kegs |
| | G.W. Horsey | ca. 1889–90 | Baskets |
| | Ward & Co. | ca. 1890–93 | Boxes |
| Seaford | Coulborn & Battey | ca. 1890–94 | Baskets |
| Townsend | John W. Naudain | ca. 1891–93 | Brooms |
| Wilmington | H.K. Fulton | ca. 1890 | Brooms and Whisks |
| | Wilmington Mfg. Company | ca. 1866–90 | General Woodenware |

| City | Company | Year | Item |
|---|---|---|---|
| **DISTRICT OF COLUMBIA** | | | |
| | Ferdinand Fender | ca. 1858–60 | Baskets |
| | F. Rosher | ca. 1858–59 | Baskets |
| | William Poulton | ca. 1843–58 | General Woodenware |
| | S. Rowe | ca. 1842–44 | Brooms |
| **GEORGIA** | | | |
| Augusta | J.J. McGuire | ca. 1865–66 | General Woodenware |
| | James Duffie | ca. 1864–70 | General Woodenware |
| Rabun Gap | Arie Carpenter | ca. 1912–35 | Bow Baskets |
| Rydal | Lyna Dysert | ca. 1920–35 | Honneysuckle Baskets |
| Savannah | Frederich Mueller | ca. 1740 | Spinning Wheels |
| **ILLINOIS** | | | |
| Aurora | Isaac P. Smith | ca. 1858–60 | Brooms |
| Champaign | Johnson & Bogardus | ca. 1857–58 | Brooms |
| Chicago | E.W. Warner | ca. 1858–59 | Brooms |
| | John Deperling | ca. 1843–44 | Baskets |
| | Charles Grey | ca. 1839–40 | Grain Cradles |
| | Charles Culver | ca. 1840 | General Woodenware |
| | Benjamin Sammons | ca. 1837–42 | General Woodenware |
| | John Brockschmidt | ca. 1843–44 | Baskets |
| | Abraham Baltz | ca. 1842–43 | General Woodenware |
| | Thomas Tucker | ca. 1839 | General Woodenware |
| | Charles Ludwig | ca. 1839–40 | General Woodenware |

| City | Company | Year | Item |
|---|---|---|---|
| Peoria | Henry Leuder | ca. 1858–59 | Baskets |
| | Fowler & Curtis | ca. 1860 | Churns, Corn Shellers |
| Quincy | Felton & Potter | ca. 1857–59 | Grain Measures |
| | N.V. Schermerhorn | ca. 1867–68 | Brooms and Wisps |
| Springfield | Lewis & Johnson | ca. 1848–50 | Churns |
| **INDIANA** | | | |
| Evansville | Brinkmayer & Harper | ca. 1878–80 | Woodenware |
| Fort Wayne | Louis Schanck | ca. 1877–78 | Baskets |
| Indianapolis | Charles Meyer | ca. 1857–60 | General Woodenware |
| | William Scheffel | ca. 1878–80 | Willowware |
| | William Metlin | ca. 1877–79 | Willowware |
| | Udell Woodenware & Ladder Co. | ca. 1878–80 | General Woodenware |
| Jeffersonville | John Wroughton | ca. 1860–62 | Willowware |
| | Hamilton Fairchild | ca. 1857–60 | Bowls |
| Madison | Alex Williams | ca. 1857–64 | Bowls |
| New Albany | Jacob Schafer | ca. 1878–80 | Baskets |
| | Joseph Schaefer | ca. 1878–79 | Baskets |
| | Peter Schaub | ca. 1878–79 | Baskets |
| Richland | George Detch | ca. 1878–80 | General Woodenware |
| Russellville | J.W. Cooper | ca. 1856–59 | Bowls |
| **IOWA** | | | |
| Dubuque | Caleb Sadler | ca. 1865–67 | Pails and Tubs |
| | Charles Converse | ca. 1864–70 | Patent Fruit Baskets |
| Franklin Center | Matthew Weil | ca. 1865 | General Woodenware |

| City | Company | Year | Item |
|---|---|---|---|
| Giard | John Hirings | ca. 1864–66 | General Woodenware |
| Iowa City | George Marquart | ca. 1866–70 | General Woodenware |
| Quasqueton | Adams & Johnson | ca. 1870 | General Woodenware |

**KANSAS**

| | | | |
|---|---|---|---|
| Kansas City | Moline Plow Co. | ca. 1870–86 | Corn Shellers |
| | Sandwich Mfg. Co. | ca. 1856–86 | Corn Shellers |

**KENTUCKY**

| | | | |
|---|---|---|---|
| Frankfort | N. Fischwenger | ca. 1868 | Baskets |
| Hindman | Carol Ritchie | ca. 1900–20 | Egg Baskets |
| Louisville | Andrew Fritz | ca. 1859–68 | Baskets |
| | Balstar Swabel | ca. 1858–59 | Baskets |
| | W. W. Talbot | ca. 1856–58 | Baskets |
| | Anthony Englehart | ca. 1857–59 | Baskets |
| | Michael Hillrich | ca. 1867–70 | Tubs and Churns |
| | Moreland & Co. | ca. 1868–69 | Washing Machines |
| | John Rentner | ca. 1867–69 | Baskets |
| | Nicholas Neff | ca. 1867–68 | Baskets |
| | Julius Sues | ca. 1868 | Willow and Woodenware |
| Macon | Nannie Sego | ca. 1910–20 | Utility Baskets |
| Vest | Bird Owsley | ca. 1890–1920 | Melon-Shaped Baskets |

**LOUISIANA**

| | | | |
|---|---|---|---|
| Gretna | Chickasaw Wood Products Co. | ca. 1882–1925 | Barrels |

| City | Company | Year | Item |
|---|---|---|---|
| New Orleans | Charles Berbusse | ca. 1867–68 | Baskets |
| | Andreas Dierkes | ca. 1859–67 | Baskets |
| | New Orleans Barrel Manufacturing Co. | ca. 1867–68 | Barrels |
| | August Goldsmith | ca. 1865–67 | Baskets |
| | G. Hobush | ca. 1865–67 | Willoware |
| | J. Williams | ca. 1859–60 | Barrels |
| | M. Bastian | ca. 1859 | Bungs and Plugs |
| | H. Huither | ca. 1867–68 | Baskets |
| | L. Wasmuth | ca. 1867 | Baskets |
| | N.F. Suerman | ca. 1866–68 | Baskets |
| | V. Biri | ca. 1865 | Baskets |
| | David Waesmuth | ca. 1865–66 | Baskets |

**MAINE**

| City | Company | Year | Item |
|---|---|---|---|
| Abbot | Phineas Weeks | ca. 1856–57 | Pails |
| Bath | George Vaughn | ca. 1867–68 | Kegs, Buckets, Barrels |
| Bridgewater | John S. Newell | ca. 1960–70 | Baskets |
| Brownfield | J.M. Brown | ca. 1856–60 | Tubs |
| Brunswick | Lunt & Wing | ca. 1855–61 | Sugar Boxes |
| Ellsworth | Austin & Chute | ca. 1856–57 | Sugar Boxes |
| Fayette | Samuel Merrill | ca. 1857 | Spools |
| | Aldon Lane | ca. 1857–58 | Pillboxes |
| Knox | Hiram Hatch | ca. 1857–58 | Pails |
| Livermore | N. Norcross | ca. 1857–60 | Pillboxes |
| Smyrna | Jerry Levi | ca. 1857–58 | Pails |

**MARYLAND**

| City | Company | Year | Item |
|---|---|---|---|
| Baltimore | Henry Christhilf | ca. 1845–46 | Cedar Buckets |

| City | Company | Year | Item |
|---|---|---|---|
|  | Spencer Rowe | ca. 1845 | Buckets, Brooms, Mats |
|  | John Dwyer | ca. 1867 | Baskets |
|  | V. Edelman | ca. 1867–68 | Boxes |
|  | John I. Sturgis | ca. 1867 | General Woodenware |
| Federalsburg | William Neale | ca. 1867–68 | Brooms |
| Towsontown | Lewis Vogle | ca. 1866–68 | Baskets |

**MASSACHUSETTS**

| City | Company | Year | Item |
|---|---|---|---|
| Boston | O. Lappan & Co. | ca. 1880–83 | Baskets |
|  | A.J. Porter | ca. 1880 | Baskets |
|  | E.O. Wires & Co. | ca. 1880–90 | Lap Boards |
|  | William McFarland | ca. 1875–82 | Cups |
|  | Crystal Rolling Pin Company | ca. 1878–80 | Rolling Pins |
|  | Highland Broom Co. | ca. 1880 | Brooms |
|  | Coombs & Pease | ca. 1879–81 | Rattan Ware |
|  | Wakefield Rattan Co. | ca. 1879–84 | Rattan Ware |
|  | F. Partheimuller | ca. 1880–81 | Baskets |
| Fall River | Cook, Bowden & Co. | ca. 1866–67 | Boxes |
|  | Lockwood & Austin | ca. 1867 | Spools |
| Hadley | Levi Dickinson | ca. 1798–1820 | Brooms |
| Hingham | Edmund Hersey | ca. 1850 | Salt and Fruit Boxes |
| Lee | Abner Taylor | ca. 1820–50 | Candlestands, Ballot Boxes |
| Leicester | L.S. Watson & Co. | ca. 1842–1952 | Wool Cards, Loom Shuttles |
| Nantucket | Charles B. Ray | ca. 1860–70 | Nantucket Baskets |
|  | Charles Coggeshall | ca. 1860 | Nantucket Baskets |

Appendix 201

| City | Company | Year | Item |
|---|---|---|---|
| | S.B. Raymond | ca. 1850–70 | Nantucket Baskets |
| | Charles B. Cox | ca. 1870 | Nantucket Baskets |
| Tyringham | Marshall Stedman | ca. 1887–1927 | Sieves |
| Washington | John King | ca. 1775 | Burl Bowls |
| West Bridgewater | Purdon Keith | ca. 1840 | Ladles, Pipkins, Leach Tubs, Noggins |
| West Mansfield | Abner Bailey | ca. 1795 | General Woodenware |
| Winchendon | Ephriam Murdock | ca. 1840 | Pails, Clothespins |
| Wrentham | Thomas Clark | ca. 1780 | Dishes, Spoons, Bowls |

**MICHIGAN**

| City | Company | Year | Item |
|---|---|---|---|
| Ada | Everett Moses & Co. | ca. 1856–57 | Bowls |
| Albion | George Cady | ca. 1856 | General Woodenware |
| Almont | Henry Reed | ca. 1860–61 | Brooms |
| Ann Arbor | Seabolt & Buell | ca. 1868–70 | Brooms |
| | Partridge & Mallory | ca. 1868–70 | Rakes, Hay Forks |
| | Charles Rodgers | ca. 1869–72 | General Woodenware |
| | Henry Fisher | ca. 1868 | Willowware |
| Batavia | Smith Dow | ca. 1860 | Brooms |
| Detroit | S. Griggs & Co. | ca. 1856–60 | Willowware |
| | Charles Parshall | ca. 1861–62 | Boxes |
| East Saginaw | C.T. Harris | ca. 1868–69 | General Woodenware |

| City | Company | Year | Item |
|---|---|---|---|
| **MINNESOTA** | | | |
| Forrestville | J.S. Perry | ca. 1865 | Spinning Wheels |
| St. Paul | Joseph Brinks | ca. 1863–64 | Barrels |
| | Augustus Palmer | ca. 1863 | Barrels |
| | F. Higham | ca. 1863–64 | Brooms |
| | Henry Stewart | ca. 1863–64 | Brooms |
| | A. Cutter & Co. | ca. 1866–67 | Barrels |
| | Brings & Goebbel | ca. 1866 | Kegs, Barrels |
| | G.W. Tapley | ca. 1867–68 | Brooms |
| | Justin Putnam | ca. 1867 | Brooms |
| | Thomas Ashton | ca. 1865–66 | Brooms |
| Winona | Doud & Sons | ca. 1866–67 | Tubs, Barrels, Firkins |
| **MISSISSIPPI** | | | |
| Enterprise | Levy, Wolverton & Co. | ca. 1866–67 | General Woodenware |
| Pine Ridge | J. Ashley | ca. 1866 | Willow and Woodenware |
| **MISSOURI** | | | |
| Alexandria | Enoch Hinkley | ca. 1867–68 | Brooms |
| Macon City | Milan & Clarkson | ca. 1868 | Brooms |
| Maysville | Simon Kail | ca. 1867–68 | Brooms |
| Savannah | William Hobson | ca. 1867–68 | Looms |
| St. Louis | Tamm & Meyer | ca. 1864–66 | Buckets and Pails |
| | William Court | ca. 1864 | Boxes |
| | Etling & Co. | ca. 1864–67 | Well Buckets |
| | John Herman | ca. 1864 | Kegs |
| | John Wich | ca. 1864–65 | Boxes |
| | John Brady | ca. 1864–65 | Brooms |
| | A. & E. Kilburn | ca. 1865 | Boxes |

| City | Company | Year | Item |
|---|---|---|---|

**NEW HAMPSHIRE**

| City | Company | Year | Item |
|---|---|---|---|
| Boscowen | Nathan Hunt | ca. 1900 | Baskets |
| Brookfield | Benich Whitfield | ca. 1890–1900 | Baskets |
| Gorham | Stephen Messer | ca. 1900–20 | Baskets |
| Haverhill | Manley Coffran | ca. 1920 | Baskets |
| Henniker | Timothy Gillette | ca. 1817–50 | Skimmers, Butter Molds, Plates |
| Jaffrey | John Eaton | ca. 1770 | Leach Tubs, Spinning Wheels, Cheese Presses |
|  | Arad Adams | ca. 1870 | Clothespins |
| Kimball | S. Warren | ca. 1865–1902 | Butter Prints, Rolling Pins, Mauls |
| Petersburough | Amzie Childs | ca. 1870–80 | Baskets |
| Plymouth | David Welch | ca. 1880 | Baskets |
| Rindge | John Prescott | ca. 1825 | Baskets |
|  | Thomas Annett | ca. 1850–70 | Spice Boxes |
|  | Richard Kimball | ca. 1860 | Clothespins |
| South Tamworth | Arthur Corliss | ca. 1860–70 | Bushel, Wood, Melon, Shaped and Wastepaper Baskets |
| Troy | Thomas Clark | ca. 1800 | Mortars, Dishes, Bowls, Spoons, and Spools |
| Wakefield | Daniel Hall | ca. 1850 | Baskets |

| City | Company | Year | Item |
|---|---|---|---|
| **NEW JERSEY** | | | |
| Allowaystown | Joseph Ecret | ca. 1860 | Baskets |
| Cassville | Archer Riley | ca. 1860–61 | Baskets |
| Cinnaminson | William Perry | ca. 1874–80 | Fruit Baskets |
| Elizabeth | E.W. Phelps | ca. 1860–62 | Beehives |
| Newark | Alexander Fuss | ca. 1860 | Baskets |
| | Fred Stegmuller | ca. 1860–63 | Boxes |
| | F. Gegenheimer | ca. 1860–61 | Buckets |
| | William Taylor | ca. 1860 | Baskets |
| Paterson | John Cutler | ca. 1860–68 | Bobbins |
| | A. Carter | ca. 1852 | Bobbins |
| | Alexander Stutz | ca. 1867 | Baskets |
| | J. & C. Andrews | ca. 1852 | Bobbins |
| Trenton | Edmund Craft | ca. 1857 | Boxes |
| | Caroline Frey | ca. 1870–72 | Baskets |
| | Jacob Sherer | ca. 1857–58 | Baskets |
| | Andrew Quinton | ca. 1860–62 | Baskets |
| Woodstown | Noah Urion | ca. 1860 | Brooms |
| **NEW YORK** | | | |
| Albany | Jacob Metzger | ca. 1864–65 | Baskets |
| Bangor | Ross, Gates & Smith | ca. 1864 | Butter Tubs |
| Brockport | E. Colby | ca. 1870–90 | Fruit Baskets |
| Carthage | Harry Farrar | ca. 1863–65 | Pails and Tubs |
| Castleton | Joan Reed | ca. 1825–42 | Willow Baskets |
| Cohoes | North & Boque | ca. 1863–64 | Bobbins, Spools, Drying Boards |

| City | Company | Year | Item |
|---|---|---|---|
| Colton | J.G. Morgan | ca. 1859–60 | Butter Tubs |
| Davenport | John Crawford | ca. 1858–61 | Washtubs |
| Dryden | G.H. Washburn | ca. 1863–65 | Clothespins |
| Dunning | J. Pardee | ca. 1859–62 | Trays |
| Eaton | Payne Truman | ca. 1863–66 | Cheese Boxes |
| Ellicott | H. Seldon | ca. 1859–60 | Pails and Tubs |
| Flushing | Henry Bennewitz | ca. 1859–60 | Baskets |
| French Creek | Jacob Havens | ca. 1858–59 | Buckets |
| Gouverneur | J.P. Fisher | ca. 1859–60 | Churns |
| Greenport | D. Hart | ca. 1859 | Baskets |
| Hunter | C.W. Burgess | ca. 1860 | Sieves |
| Knox | Nathan Crary | ca. 1806–1906 | Pillboxes |
| Northampton | Jacob Phillips | ca. 1859–60 | Measures |
| New Lebanon | Abiathar Babbit<br>Ebenezer Cooley<br>John Farrington | ca. 1811<br>ca. 1806–16<br>ca. 1800 | Dippers<br>Shaker Boxes<br>Shaker Boxes |
| New York | Thomas Day, Jr.<br>Barnard Andrews<br>L.H. Mace & Co. | 19th century<br>19th century<br>ca. 1860–1900 | Bandboxes<br>Bandboxes<br>General Woodenware |
| Pound Ridge | Selleck Basket Factory | ca. 1840–1920 | Grain, Bushel, Egg and Clam Baskets |
| Shaverton | Edwin Russell | ca. 1890–1900 | Churns, Keelers |
| South Butler | Hibbard Basket Factory | ca. 1900 | Bushel, Egg and Utility Baskets |

| City | Company | Year | Item |
|---|---|---|---|
| Southampton | Natheniel Dominy IV | | Platters, Candle Boxes |
| | Natheniel Dominy V | | Reels, Mortars |
| Staten Island | John Merrell | ca. 1840 | Fruit Baskets |
| | Obidiah Jones | ca. 1860 | Oyster Baskets |
| | James Morgan | ca. 1842 | Oyster, Bread, and Fruit Baskets |
| Towanda | J.C. Titus | ca. 1859–60 | Baskets |
| Whitestown | Ellis Watson & Co. | ca. 1859–61 | Pails, Tubs, Churns |

**NORTH CAROLINA**

| City | Company | Year | Item |
|---|---|---|---|
| Creswell | A. Alexander | ca. 1880–85 | Boxes |
| Durham | Lee & Wheeler | ca. 1883–84 | General Woodenware |
| Fayetteville | C.S. Taylor | ca. 1882–83 | General Woodenware |
| | R.M. Nimocks | ca. 1883–85 | Oak Barrels |
| Goldsboro | F.C. Overman | ca. 1880–83 | Boxes, Barrels |
| Greensboro | R.W. Brooks | ca. 1882–86 | Boxes |
| Mount Olive | F. Overman | ca. 1884–85 | Boxes, Baskets |
| New Bern | Jones Mfg. Co. | ca. 1883–84 | Barrels |
| | Elm City Barrel Factory | ca. 1884–87 | Barrels |
| Ruben | James Moore | ca. 1883–84 | Barrels and Boxes |
| Salem | C.F. Jenkins | ca. 1884–87 | Brooms |
| | Spaugh Brothers | ca. 1883–85 | Tobacco Boxes |
| Scuppernog | T.J. Basnight | ca. 1884–86 | Boxes |
| Southern Pines | Fred Chandler | ca. 1880–90 | Baskets |

| City | Company | Year | Item |
|---|---|---|---|
| Statesville | C.L. Wagoner | ca. 1881–84 | Buckets, Tubs |
| Warsaw | T.P. Pierce | ca. 1884–87 | Baskets |
| Wilmington | Harrison Planing Mills | ca. 1896 | Fruit Baskets |
|  | Richard Harris | ca. 1860 | General Woodenware |

**OHIO**

| City | Company | Year | Item |
|---|---|---|---|
| Berea | J.W. Fairchild | ca. 1850–60 | Wooden Bowls |
|  | Jonathan Pickard | ca. 1850–53 | Wooden Bowls |
| Bellaire | William Hall | ca. 1850 | Brooms |
| Bryan | Joseph Barrons | ca. 1850–55 | General Woodenware |
|  | William Honnet | ca. 1850–55 | General Woodenware |
| Chandler | Thomas Murphy | ca. 1853 | Wool Cards |
| Cincinnati | J. P. Ottignan | ca. 1850–55 | Baskets |
|  | J.F. Barnholt | ca. 1849–52 | Bandboxes |
|  | William Friedman | ca. 1850–55 | Bandboxes |
| Cuba | E. Hannon | ca. 1853–54 | Baskets |
| Deerfield | William Cox | ca. 1852–54 | Baskets |
| Farrington | J.H. & L.B. Wolcott | ca. 1850–54 | Cheese Boxes |
| Gates Mills | W.J. Hilt | ca. 1852–53 | Cheese Boxes |
| Harmer | Harmer Pail Factory | ca. 1852–56 | Pails |
| Lindonville | Dan Palmer | ca. 1851–53 | Cheese Boxes |
| Lake County | Hiram Pease | ca. 1850–90 | Salts, Sugar Bowls, Darning Knobs, Thimble and Spool Holders |

| City | Company | Year | Item |
|---|---|---|---|
| Munson | H. Seeland | ca. 1852–54 | Churns |
| Painesville | J.C. Brown | ca. 1900–20 | Spice Boxes |
| Ripley | L. Sayres | ca. 1850–60 | Wool Cards |
| Rome | J.O. Miller | ca. 1853–54 | Cheese Boxes |
| Rootstown | Solomon Finch | ca. 1855 | Baskets |
| Solon | Bull & Tucker<br>L. Chamberlain | ca. 1853–55<br>ca. 1848–60 | Cheese Boxes<br>Cheese Boxes |
| Streetsboro | Henry Springer | ca. 1853 | Baskets |
| Troy | L. Williams | ca. 1852–53 | Baskets |
| Upper Sandusky | J. Schwartz | ca. 1853–55 | General Woodenware |
| Wellsville | Horace Fuller | ca. 1850 | Brooms |
| West Unity | Cass Jones | ca. 1852–55 | General Woodenware |
| Zoar | Conrad Dienman | ca. 1820–60 | Spinning Wheels |

**PENNSYLVANIA**

| City | Company | Year | Item |
|---|---|---|---|
| Berks County | Henrich Bucher | ca. 1800 | Baskets |
| Downing's Field | Moses Coates | ca. 1803 | Patent Apple Parers |
| Fallston | Miner & Champlin | ca. 1847–50 | Buckets |
| Harrisburg | Robert Bleyer<br>Jacob Waters | ca. 1867–68<br>ca. 1867 | Baskets<br>Brooms |
| Lawsville | Russel Southworth | ca. 1860–1900 | Churns, Tubs, and Firkins |
| McKeesport | N. Lovely | ca. 1847–48 | Bandboxes |

| City | Company | Year | Item |
|---|---|---|---|
| Philadelphia | H. Barnes | ca. 1850–60 | Bandboxes |
| | McLoughlin & Diffendorfer | ca. 1870 | Brooms, Willowware |
| | David Trotter | ca. 1789 | Bread Peels |
| | William Savery | ca. 1775 | Pastry Boards, Salt-Boxes, Sugar Bowls, Rolling Pins, Trays |
| | Issac Ashton | ca. 1778 | Knife Boxes, Cuspidors |
| | David Evans | ca. 1770 | Cuspidors, Chopping Boards, Towel Rollers |
| | Samuel Matthews | ca. 1800 | Wig Boxes |
| Reading | John Schefeler | ca. 1867 | Baskets |
| | John Zieber | ca. 1866–68 | Brooms |
| | H.B. Scherer | ca. 1866–67 | Pails |

**RHODE ISLAND**

| City | Company | Year | Item |
|---|---|---|---|
| Exeter | Joshua Boss | ca. 1856–68 | Rakes |
| Fiskville | Stephen Potter | ca. 1867–68 | Bobbins |
| Pawtucket | Walter Gardner | ca. 1868 | Brooms |
| Providence | Emery Cushman | ca. 1843–56 | Boxes |
| | J.C. Lee & Co. | ca. 1843–45 | Boxes |
| | W.B. Dean | ca. 1849–50 | Boxes |
| | C. Gilbert | ca. 1849 | Baskets |
| | Miles & Maxon | ca. 1856–57 | Willow Baskets |
| | J.P. Haskin & Son | ca. 1856–68 | Kegs and Boxes |
| | John Wood | ca. 1867–68 | Dippers |
| | Smith & Fuller | ca. 1843 | Brooms |
| Scituate | Josiah Whitaker | ca. 1856–57 | Spools |

| City | Company | Year | Item |
|---|---|---|---|

### SOUTH CAROLINA

| | | | |
|---|---|---|---|
| Charlestown | Berbusse & Berkmeyer | ca. 1869–70 | Baskets |

### TENNESEE

| | | | |
|---|---|---|---|
| Gatlingburg | Mac McCarter | ca. 1910–30 | Market Baskets |
| | Lydia Whaley | ca. 1900–25 | Willow Egg Baskets |
| Memphis | Chickasaw Wood Products Company | ca. 1882–1925 | Boxes, Barrels |
| | Wheeler, Pickens & Co. | ca. 1867–68 | Brooms |
| | F. Heit | ca. 1869–70 | Baskets |
| Nashville | W.R. McFarland | ca. 1860 | Boxes |
| | John T. Brown | ca. 1860–61 | Willowware |
| | J.W. Wilson | ca. 1860–61 | Willowware |
| | Francis Brunker | ca. 1860 | Willowware |
| Shelbyville | Burns, O'Neal & Co. | ca. 1857–58 | General Woodenware |
| | S. Doak & Co. | ca. 1857 | Buckets |

### TEXAS

| | | | |
|---|---|---|---|
| Coleman | ——Gilland | ca. 1880 | Churns |
| Lexington | Joseph Jackson & Sons | ca. 1840–1920 | Ox Yokes, Spinning Wheels |

### UTAH

| | | | |
|---|---|---|---|
| Salt Lake City | Job Smith | ca. 1869–71 | Baskets |
| | E.D. Wooley | ca. 1869–71 | Pails |

Appendix 210

Appendix 211

| City | Company | Year | Item |
|------|---------|------|------|
| **VERMONT** | | | |
| Arlington | Benjamin Safford | ca. 1868–69 | Washboards |
| | Billings, Hurl & Co. | ca. 1856 | Washboards |
| Athens | Dunham & Upton | ca. 1868–69 | Ox Bows |
| Barnet | James Warden | ca. 1868 | Rakes |
| | A.B. Norris | ca. 1867–68 | Bobbins |
| Bloomfield | Jackson, Perkins & Co. | ca. 1867–68 | Sugar Boxes |
| Bradford | D.R. Aldrich | ca. 1868 | Kits |
| Burlington | K.P. Kidder | ca. 1865–68 | Beehives |
| Danby | N. Kelly | ca. 1868 | Cheese Boxes |
| Dover | S.H. Sherman | ca. 1867–68 | Sap Tubs |
| East Poultney | Charles Ripley | ca. 1867–68 | Tubs, Pails, and Boxes |
| Granville | Newman Rice | ca. 1913 | Bowls |
| Hinesborough | Rufus Patrick | ca. 1868 | Cheese Presses |
| Island Pond | I.C. Averill | ca. 1868–69 | Pillboxes |
| Marshfield | L.T. Kinney | ca. 1850 | Bowls, Pig Troughs |
| Mechanicsville | Johnson & Graves | ca. 1867–68 | Butter and Cheese Boxes |
| | Benjamin Priest | ca. 1856 | Trays |
| Montgomery | L. Hendrex | ca. 1856 | Butter Tubs |
| Mt. Holly | N.A. Holton & Co. | ca. 1856–57 | Tubs and Bowls |
| Peacham | Ben Thresher | ca. 1845 | Water Tubs |

| City | Company | Year | Item |
|---|---|---|---|
| Searsbury | C. Aaron Pike<br>Duane & Stanley | ca. 1856–57<br>ca. 1867–68 | Cheese Presses<br>Grain Measures |
| Sharon | Moses Flanders | ca. 1868 | Washing Machines |
| Springfield | Smith, Mason & Co. | ca. 1867–68 | Rolling Pins |
| Westminster | Olin Stevens<br>William Gage | ca. 1867–69<br>ca. 1868 | Baskets<br>Baskets |
| Weston | Rufus Simmons | ca. 1867–69 | Bowls |
| Wolcott | Potter & Abell | ca. 1869 | Pillboxes |

**VIRGINIA**

| City | Company | Year | Item |
|---|---|---|---|
| Alexandria | H.E. Smith | ca. 1870 | Brooms |
| Fairfax County | Jonathan Constable | ca. 1870 | Brooms |
| Oldrag | Silas Nicholson | ca. 1900–30 | Market Baskets |
| Norfolk | Alexander Hall<br>William P. Henneley<br>I.S. Bixby | ca. 1866–67<br>ca. 1866–68<br>ca. 1866 | Grain Measures<br>Willowware<br>General Woodenware |
| Richmond | Philip Webber | ca. 1866–67 | Willowware |

**WEST VIRGINIA**

| City | Company | Year | Item |
|---|---|---|---|
| Fulton | John Crouse | ca. 1851–52 | Baskets |
| Pendleton | Levi Eye | ca. 1880–1928 | Egg and Market Baskets |
| Wheeling | John Andrews<br>Anthony Gollner | ca. 1867–68<br>ca. 1867 | Baskets<br>Baskets |

Appendix 213

| City | Company | Year | Item |
|---|---|---|---|

**WISCONSIN**

| | | | |
|---|---|---|---|
| Beloit | Beloit Willow Works | ca. 1865–66 | Willow Hampers, Clothes Baskets, Cradles, and Market Baskets |
| | Hatch & Rodgers | ca. 1865–66 | Baskets |
| Madison | Gibson & Wymond | ca. 1867–68 | Barrels, Kegs |
| Manitowoc | Frank Feuker | ca. 1868 | Bonnet Boxes |
| Milwaukee | Badger Washboard Co. | ca. 1867–68 | Washboards |
| | J. Fischer | ca. 1865–68 | Baskets |
| | C.F. Rann | ca. 1865–68 | Baskets |
| | A.H. Filner | ca. 1866 | Washing Machines |
| | Mann Brothers | ca. 1865–66 | General Woodenware |
| | Judd & Hiiles | ca. 1867 | Baskets |
| | J. Graham | ca. 1865–66 | Brooms |
| | J.A. Jaeger | ca. 1867 | Boxes |
| | Charles F. Raun | ca. 1868–69 | Baskets |

# Bibliography

## General Sources

Andrews, Edward D. *The Community Industries of the Shakers.* Albany: University of the State of New York, 1932.

Bobart, H.H. *Basketwork Through the Ages.* London and New York: Oxford University Press, 1936.

Bowles, Ella Shannon. *Homespun Handicrafts.* New York: J.B. Lippincott Co., 1931.

Card, Devere. *The Use of Burl in America.* Utica: Munson, Williams, Proctor Institute, 1971.

Crosby, Everett V. *Baskets, Signs and Silver of Old Time Nantucket.* Nantucket: Inquier and Mirror Press, 1940.

Cummings, Abbott Lowell, ed. *Rural Household Inventories.* Boston: The Society for the Preservation of New England Antiquities, 1964.

Deane, Samuel. *The New England Farmer or Georgical Dictionary.* Worcester, 1790.

Dolan, J.R. *The Yankee Pedlars of Early America.* New York: Bramhall House, 1946.

Dow, George Francis. *Arts and Crafts in New England.* New York: DaCapo Press, 1967.

Drown, William. *The Compendium of Agriculture or the Farmer's Friend.* Providence: Field and Maxey, 1824.

Earle, Alice Morse. *Home Life in Colonial Days.* New York: Macmillan Co., 1898.

Eaton, Allen. *Handicrafts of New England.* New York: Harper, 1947.

———. *Handicrafts of the Southern Highlands.* New York: Russell Sage Foundation, 1937.

Gould, Mary Earle. *Early American Woodenware.* Rutland: Charles E. Tuttle Co., 1971.

———. *The Early American House*. New York: Medrill, McBride and Co., 1949.

Harris, Jay. *God's Country*. Connecticut: Pequot Press, 1971.

Hazen, Edward. *Hazen's Panorama of Professions and Trades*. Philadelphia: Uriah Hunt, 1837.

Humphreys, James. *Gleanings from the Most Celebrated Books on Husbandry, etc*. Philadelphia, 1803.

James and Johnson. *Remarks on the Manufacturing of Maple Syrup*. Philadelphia, 1790.

Kilby, Kenneth. *The Cooper and His Trade*. Fernhill House, New York, 1972.

Kovel, Ralph, and Kovel, Terry. *American Country Furniture, 1780–1875*. New York: Crown Publishers, Inc., 1965.

Lantz, Louise K. *Old American Kitchenware, 1725–1925*. Hanover: Nelson, Everybodys Press, 1970.

Lichten, Frances. *Folk Art of Rural Pennsylvania*. New York: Charles Scribner's Sons, 1946.

Lismer, Marjorie. *Seneca Splint Basketry*. Chilocco: the author, 1941.

McAfee, Mary J. *The Pine Needle Book*. New York: Pine Needle Publishing Co., 1911.

Mace, L.H. and Co. *Woodenware Catalog*. 1883. Reprint. Princeton: The Pyne Press, 1971.

Morse, John D. ed. *Country Cabinetwork and Simple City Furniture*. Charlottesville: University of Virginia Press, 1970.

Phipps, Frances. *Colonial Kitchens, Their Furnishings and Their Gardens*. New York: Hawthorne Books, 1972.

Pinto, Edward H. *Treen and Other Wooden Bygones*. London: G. Bell and Sons, 1969.

Rawson, Marion Nicholl. *Handwrought Ancestors*. New York: E.P. Dutton and Co., 1936.

Reinert, Guy F. *Pennsylvania German Splint and Straw Baskets*. Plymouth Meeting: C. Naamen Keyser, 1946.

Speare, Elizabeth. *Life in Colonial America*. New York: Random House, 1963.

Winchester, Alice, ed. *The Antiques Treasury*. New York: E.P. Dutton and Co., 1959.

Woodstock, Lenoir. *Basketry*. Independence: Herald House, 1960.

## Magazine Articles

Bacon, J. Earle. "Washing Machines." *The Chronicle of the Early American Industries Association*, April 1942.

Blodgett, W.P. "Gum Books." *The Chronicle of the Early American Industries Association*, August 1939.

Borcourt, Janet. "American Woodenware for the Casual Collector." *Antiques Magazine*, December 1951.

Brower, Leslie W. "The Pillbox Industry." *The Chronicle of the Early American Industry Association*, December 1939.

Dreppard, Carl W. "Origins of Pennsylvania Folk Art." *Antiques Magazine*, February 1940.

Frary, I.T. "Stagecoach Luggage." *Antiques Magazine*, August 1940.

Guldbeck, Per E. "Traditional Soap Making on the Frontier." *The Chronicle of the Early American Industries Association*, June 1963.

Gould, Mary Earle. "The Scope of Woodenware and the Part It Played in History." *Old Time New England*, October 1944.

──────. "Wooden Bowls." *The Chronicle of the Early American Industries Association*, July 1937.

──────. "Butter Molds and Prints." *The Chronicle of the Early American Industries Association*, March 1938.

──────. "Laundry Emplements." *The Chronicle of the Early American Industries Association*, April 1939.

──────. "Early New England Woodenware." *Antiques Magazine*, February 1937.

──────. "Mortars, Pestles and their Uses." *The Chronicle of the Early American Industries Association*, December 1961.

──────. "Branding and Stamping Tools." *The Chronicle of the Early American Industries Association*, March 1961.

──────. "The Curious History of Our Tin Graters." *Antiques Journal*, September 1972.

──────. "The Burl and Its Uses." *Antiques Magazine*, October 1939.

──────. "The Smoothing Board." *The Chronicle of the Early American Industries Association*, September 1938.

──────. "The Useful Bucket." *Spinning Wheel*, October 1972.

———. "Horse Hair Sieves." *The Chronicle of the Early American Industries Association*, September 1940.

Gove, William S. "Wooden Bowls." *Vermont Life* 25, no. 4.

Hynson, Garret. "Maine Butter Molds." *The Chronicle of the Early American Industries Association*, April 1942.

Hynson, Garret, and Nash, S. "Design In Yankee Butter Molds." *Antiques Magazine*, February 1942.

Johnson, Lawrence A. "Battle of the Baskets." *The Chronicle of the Early American Industries Association*, September 1962.

———. "The Niddy Noddy." *The Chronicle of the Early American Industries Association*, July 1958.

Larsen, Peter. "Butter Stamps and Molds." *Antiques Magazine*, July 1939.

McClees, John. "Basket Making." *Antiques Magazine*, May 1931.

Miniter, Edith. "When Women's Work Was Never Done." *Antiques Magazine*, September 1926.

———. "When Treen Ware Was the Ware." *Antiques Magazine*, December 1930.

Mitchell, Robert. "Apple Pickers, Parers, Corers and Slicers." *The Chronicle of the Early American Industries Association*, June 1964.

Robacker, Earl F. "Wooden Boxes of German Pennsylvania." *Antiques Magazine*, February 1952.

Romaine, Lawrence, B. "Purdon Keith, Cooper of West Bridgwater, Massachusetts." *The Chronicle of the Early American Industries Association*, April 1952.

———. "Basket Making." *The Chronicle of the Early American Industries Association*, March 1939.

Sprague, Wiliam B. "Flax Dressing by Hand." *The Chronicle of the Early American Industries Association*, May 1936.

———. "A Collection of American Implements." *The Chronicle of the Early American Industries Association*, September 1935.

———. "The Cooper." *The Chronicle of the Early American Industries Association*, June 1938.

Watkins, Malcom. "The Early American Domestic Machine." *Antiques Magazine*, February 1940.

Whittemore, Edwin C. "Graters and Strainers." *Spinning Wheel*, November 1966.
Whittemore, Georgina Y. "Wooden Household Devices." *The Chronicle of the Early American Industries Association*, December 1961.

# Index

Alden, John, 51
Animal transportation box, 36
Annett, Thomas, 135
Apple butter stirrer, 171
Apple grinder, 171–172
Apple parer, 73–74
Apple picker, 170
Apple slicer, 74
Armes and Dallam, 96–97
Ashton, Isaac, 90, 139

Babbit, Abiathas, 153
Bag stamps, 188
Bannock boards, 77
Barnes, Henry, 125
Barrels, 54, 173
Basket maker's stool, 8
Basket molds, 7–8
Baskets, 3–48
  cornshuck, 47
  dating, 4
  decline in style, 4
  decoration, 8
  factory made, 10
  honeysuckle vine, 47
  materials, 4
  nesting, 23
  pine needle, 46
  rattan, 47
  splint, 5–33
  straw, 41–45
  sweet grass, 46
  willow, 34–40
Bed baskets, 12
Bed pans, 139
Bed wrenches, 138

Bee finder's box, 185
Beehives, 44–45
Beecher Basket Company, 24
Bee skep, 44–45
Beetle, 107
Betty lamp stand, 148
Bobbins, 109, 110, 117
Bonnet basket
  sweet grass, 46
  willow, 36
Bootjacks, 142
Boston Wooden Box Manufactory, 63
Bottle corkers, 88
Bottles, 88
Bowls
  bread, 70, 78
  butter, 70, 159
  cheese drainer, 70
  chopping, 71
  construction of, 69
  determining use of, 70–71
  eating, 84
  grease, 70
  milk, 70
  punch, 93
  sizes of, 69
  spice, 62, 91
  sugar, 90–91
  wash, 137
Bowl scrapers, 159
Boxes
  ballot, 130
  band, 124–125
  bureau, 127
  butter, 133

## Index

bride's, 125–126
candle, 128–129
cash, 130–131
cheese, 55, 133, 168–169
comb, 141
cookie, 128
cottonwood, 130
decorated, 124–131
gum, 128
herb, 133–134
knife, 146
lather, 130
meal, 133–134
pantry, 126–127
pencil, 129–130
pie, 83
pill, 136
pumice, 146
salt, 76
Shaker, 132, 134–135
snuff, 141
spice, 55, 134
sugar, 133–134
techniques of manufacture, 53–54, 132–133
tinder, 141
trinket, 127
utility, 132–136
watch, 141
Braid looms, 119
Bread baskets, 41–42
Bread boards, 79
Bread troughs, 78
Brooms, 147–148
"Brose" spoons, 89
Brown, J. C., 135, 169
Buckets
apple butter, 171
candy, 148
flour, 151
grease, 189
sap, 175–176
suction, 150
storage, 148–149
sugar, 148
techniques of manufacture, 148–149, 151
water, 150–151
Bucking tubs, 110–111
Burl, 52, 84
Bushel baskets, 24
Butter dishes, 89–90
Butter knives, 89
Butter molds, 161–163
Butter paddles, 159
Butter prints, 161–162
Butter spade, 160
Butter tamps, 160
Butter worker, 160
Buttons, 122


Cake boards, 80
Candle dippers, 146
Candle mold, 146
Candlesticks, 143
Cane heads, 143
Canteens, 189
Cap baskets
sweet grass, 46
willow, 36
Cap stands, 142
Carriage wheel shields, 43
"Cat," 57
Chamber pot, 138–139
Charcoal sieves, 13–14
Chargers, 86
Checkerboards, 145
Cherry pitters, 75
Cheese baskets, 25
Cheese drainers, 165–167
Cheese ladder, 167
Cheese plane, 93–94
Cheese press, 167–168
Cheese workers, 167
Chicken nesting box, 40
Chip baskets, 13
Chopping board, 72

Index **223**

Chopping tray, 71
Church offering plate, 42
Churns, 156-159
  barrel, 156-157
  pump, 159
  rocking, 157
  swing, 159
  wig-wag, 159
Cider cheese cutters, 172
Cider funnel, 173
Cider press, 172
Cider press rack, 172
Clam baskets, 32
Clam rollers, 185
Clark, Thomas, 89
Clock reel, 110
Clothes baskets
  splint, 11
  willow, 36
Clothes drying racks, 101
Clothes hampers
  splint, 11
  straw, 45
  willow, 36
Clothes horse, 101
Clothesline winder, 100
Clothes maul, 98
Clothespins, 100
Clothes pounder, 98-99
Clothes tongs, 100
Coal baskets, 14
Coates, Moses, 73
Cobweb fruit drying rack, 18
Codding, Joseph, 11, 25, 31
Converse, Charles, 24
Cook, David, 10
Cookie prints, 79-80
Cooley, Ebenezer, 135
Cooper
  butt, 51
  dry, 51
  methods employed by, 52-54
  rundlet, 51
  slack, 51
  tight, 51
  white, 51
Coombs, 184
Cooper's adze, 52
Corliss, Arthur, 14, 29
Cornsheller, 183
Cradles baskets
  splint, 12
  straw, 43
  willow, 38
Crary, Nathan, 132-133, 136
Crawford, John, 97
Cribbage boards, 144
Cross hatch weaving, 5-6
Croze, 54
Cups, 88
  egg, 72
Curd breaker, 165
Curd knife, 165
Cuspidor, 139

Darning knobs, 122
Davis, Hannah, 125
Davis, Jacob and Son, 153, 155
Day, Thomas, J., 125
Dienman, Conrad, 113
Dippers, 153-154
Dish drainer, 145
Dolly pin, 98
Dominy, Nathaniel, I, 90
Dominy, Nathaniel, IV, 86, 128
Dominy, Nathaniel, V, 61
Dough knives, 79
Doughnut cutters, 81
Downes, John, 83
Drawknife, 5, 52
Drying boards, 103-104
  bosom, 103
  skirt, 103-104
  sleeve, 104
Drying racks, fruit, 170-171
Dysart, Lena, 47

Easter eggs, 145
Eaton, John, 95, 110, 168

Eel traps, 31
Eells, Henry, 176
Egg baskets
  Kentucky, 26
  splint, 26
  straw, 45
  willow, 39
Eggbeaters, 59
Egg cups, 92
Embroidery yarn holders, 123
Evans, David, 137, 139
Extension rack, 102
Eye, Levi, 26

Fairchild, Hamilton, 84
Farrington, John, 135
Featherbed basket, 13
Featherbed smoothers, 138
Feed bags, 27
Feed box, 184
Field baskets, 22–24
Fills, 6
"Finger," 113
Finish split, 6
Fish baskets, 32
Fishing Creels
  splint, 32
  willow, 40
Fish traps, 32
Flails, 181
Flatware, 52
Flax, 105
Flax baskets
  splint, 14
  willow, 36
Flax brake, 105–106
Flax wheel, 109–110
Fleece, 112
Flip, 59
Flytraps, 147
Follers, 167–168
Food storage hampers
  splint, 18–19
  straw, 45

Foot warmers, 139
Forks, 89
Forks, farm, 180
  barley, 180
  potato, 180
Frisian carving, 80
Froe, 5, 54
Fruit baskets
  Delaware, 24
  splint, 24
  star, 24
  willow, 36
Fruit drying baskets
  splint, 17–18
  straw, 42
Fruit drying trays
  cornshuck, 47
  splint, 17–18
  straw, 42
  wood, 86
Fruit gathering baskets
  straw, 45
  willow, 38
Fuller, Edmund, 150
Funnels
  splint, 19
  wood, 75

"Gallus" frames, 118–119
Gambrels, 188
"Gape and Swaller," 58
Gilland, ———, 157
Gillette, Timothy, 156
Glasses, 88
Gingerbread prints, 80
Goblets, 88
Goose baskets, 27
Grain measures, 183–184
Gridirons, 56
Gum books, 128

Hairpins, 138
Handles, in basketry, 6
Hanging hooks, 188

Index **225**

Hasty pudding, 58
Hasty pudding spoon, 58
Hatchel, 107
Havens, Jacob, 151
Hay crooks, 181
Hay drag, 180
Herb trays, 184-185
Hexagon weaving, 6-7
Hibbard Basket Co., 20
Hoops, 167
Hot plates
  cornshuck, 42
  wood, 93
Husking pins, 182

Ice cream freezers, 75
Indian baskets, 3
Indian pack, 33
Inkwells, 139

Jackson, Joseph and Sons, 186-187, 113
Jigger, 52

Keelers, 155-156
Kegs
  oyster, 190
  rum, 190
  techniques of manufacture, 54, 152, 190
  water, 152-190
Keith, Purdon, 95-155
Kimball, Warren, 98
Kinney, L. T., 184
Kits, 184
Knife tray, 90
"Knot," 110, 114

Ladles, 89, 153
Lamp base, 143
Lap board, 122-123
Lard squeezers, 69
Lathe, 52-53
Laundry baskets

rattan, 47
willow, 36
Leach barrels, 95
Lehn George, 88, 92, 122
Lemon squeezers, 73
Loom basket, 16
Lossets, 85
Lye, 95
Lye tub, 95

Mace, L. H. and Co., 29, 35, 36, 39, 65, 67, 69, 72, 75, 79, 86, 89, 90, 93, 97, 101, 102, 123, 133, 134, 137, 149, 150, 152, 153, 155, 159, 160, 163, 179, 180, 184
Malby, Fowler and Son, 130
Mallet, 179
Mandrel lathe, 53
Manning, Aaron, 107
Maple sugar molds, 177
Maple syrup troughs, 175
Market baskets
  splint, 29-30
  willow, 39
Marle, Mark, 137
Marzipan molds, 81
Mashers, 72
Masticators, 67
Mather, Joseph, 143
Matthews, Samuel, 141-142
Mauls, 179
Meat grinders, 68
Meat pounders, 67
Melon-shaped baskets, 29-30
Mending baskets
  pine needle, 47
  splint, 16
  willow, 35
Milking stool, 191
Mitchin boxes, 18-19
Mortar and pestle, 60-61
Moses, Walter and Co., 20
Mouse traps, 149
Mugs, 86

Murdock, Ephraim, 100

Nails
  cut, 53
  handwrought, 53
  wire, 53
Nantucket baskets, 39
Napkin rings, 92
Needle boxes, 121–122
Niagara Pail and Tub Factory, 97, 176
Nicholson, Silas, 30
Niddy noddy, 113–114
Noggins, 9, 87
North and Boque, 103, 117
Nut gathering basket, 38–39

Oakland Box and Barrel Company, 173
Ohl & Hanschild, 144
Osborn, Samuel and Jonathan, 122
Osier, 38
Owsley, Bird, 30
Ox drag shoes, 188
Ox muzzle, 27
Oyster baskets, 32

Pack baskets
  splint, 32–33
  willow, 40
Palette paddles, 183
Pease, Hiram, 93, 121, 122
Peels, bread, 81
Philadelphia Ornamental Wood Co., 145
Phillips, Jacob, 184
Pie crimpers, 81
Pie lifters, 81
Pigeon baskets, 28
Pigeon boxes, 185
Piggins, 155
Pipe tray, 140
Plaiting, 5
Plates, 85
Platters, 86

Pokes, animal, 187
Pomace rake, 172
Porringers, 84–85, 88
Pot hooks, 56
Powder horns, 143
Powdering tubs, 68

Quilling wheel, 117
Quills, 117

Raisin seeders, 75
Rakes, 180
Ripple combs, 105
Riving chisel, 5
Rivings, defined, 5
Rolling pins, 79
Ross, Gates and Smith, 160
Ruggles, 188
Rundlets, 190

Salt boxes, 76
Salts, 91
Samp mortars, 191
Sanders, 140
Sap carriers, 176
Sauerkraut stompers, 73
Sausage stuffers, 68–69
Savery, William, 76, 79
Scales, butter, 160
Schiene Korbe, 22
School baskets, 35
Scoops
  apple butter, 171
  blueberry, 189
  butter, 159
  candy, 148
  cranberry, 189
  flour, 77
  maple, 176–177
  soft soap, 96
  two-way, 171
  winnowing, 181
Scotch hands, 160
Scrubbing sticks, 96, 103

## Index

Scutching knife, 106
Seal boxes, 141
Selleck Basket Works, 24, 32
Serviettes, 92
Sewing birds, 120
Sheep stamps, 188
Shovels, 179–180
  grain, 179–180
  snow, 180
Shtrow-Karab, 41
Shuttles, 117–118
Sieves, 64
Sifters, 65, 77
Silliman Manufacturing Co., 139
Skarnes, 117
Skeins, 110, 114
Skimmers, 156
Smoothing boards, 102
Smoothing sticks, 102
Soap dishes, 137
Soap sticks, 95–96
Soap tub, 95
Soft soap, 95
Soft soap barrels, 96
"Sow and Pigs," 61
Sower's baskets
  splint, 21
  straw, 44
Spatulas, 57
Speed boy, 113
Spice cannisters, 63
Spice grinder, 61
Spice mill, 61
Spice storage chest, 62–63
Spigots, 75
Spiles, 175
Spindles, 113
Splint, 5
Splint baskets, techniques of manufacture, 5–10
Splints, 5
Spool holders, 121
Spools, 117
Spoon holders, 89

Spoons, 88–89
Spoonwood, 89
Springerle boards, 80
Spring pole lathe, 52–53
Staff, 181
Stamping machines, 145
Steak mauls, 67
Stedman, Marshall, 64–65
Stirrers, 57–58
Striped wood, 144
Sugar boxes, 90–91
Sweep mills, 191
Swifts, 114–115
Swiglers, 190
Swingle, 181
Swingling block, 106–107
Swingling knife, 106
Swizzle, 59–60
Swizzle sticks, 60
Syrup jug, 93

Table mats, 93
Tankards, 86–87
Tapelooms, 118–119
Taylor, Abner, 130, 167, 143
Testers, butter, 160
Thimble baskets, 47
Thimble holders, 121
Thimbles, 120–121
Thresher, Benjamin, 153
Toddy, 59, 87
Toddy sticks, 59
Toothpick holders, 93
Tow, 107
Towel arms, 102
Towel rollers, 137
Trays, 86
Trenchers, 85
Trivets, 57
Troughs, 184
Truman, Payne, 169
Tubs
  bleach, 99–100
  butter, 160

corn shelling, 182
dish washing, 145
dye, 100
sour cream, 156
sugar storage, 177
wash, 97
water, 152–153

Urns, 91
Utility baskets
 splint, 19
 sweet grass, 46
 willow, 36

Vanavery, Daniel, 33
Veneer, 53–54
Vases
 honeysuckle, 48
 wood, 144
Vegetable slicers, 66
Voiders, 94

Wall pipe racks, 140
Washboards, 96–97
Washing machines, 99
Wastepaper baskets, 14
Water coolers, 153
Watson, L. S. and Co., 118
Webster, Joseph, 86
Whaley, Aunt Lydia, 39

Whatnot baskets, 36
Wheat riddle, 21
Wheel driver, 113
Whetstone holders, 191
Whips, egg and cream, 148
Wicker, 34
Wig boxes, 141–142
Willow "whips," 34
Wilson, Jehiel, 151
Winnowing baskets, 21
Winnowing fans
 splint, 21–22
 splint and willow, 38
Winnowing sieve, 22
Wooden medals, 145
Woodenware
 dating, 53, 55
 decoration, 52, 55
 techniques of manufacture, 52–54
Wood baskets, 13
Wool baskets, 14–15
Wool cards, 112
Wool spinning wheels, 113

Yokes
 goat, 187
 goose, 187
 ox, 186–187
 shoulder, 176
 turkey, 187